Janet Gonzalez-Mena

and

Dianne Widmeyer Eyer

Infancy and Caregiving

MAYFIELD PUBLISHING COMPANY

Library of Congress Catalog Card Number: 79-91838
International Standard Book Number: 0-87484-515-7

Manufactured in the United States of America
Mayfield Publishing Company
285 Hamilton Avenue, Palo Alto, California 94301

This book was set in VIP Souvenir Light by CBM Type and was
printed and bound by the George Banta Company. Sponsoring
editor was Robert W. Erhart and Maggie Cutler supervised
editing. Nancy Sears designed the book and art work is by
Mary Burkhardt. Michelle Hogan supervised production. Cover
design is by Joan Brown and cover photo by Michael
Rothstein/Jeroboam.

CONTENTS

It is a joy for me to have been given the opportunity to write this foreword to *Infancy and Caregiving,* a book that so sensitively represents my life's work on adult-infant interaction.

I recall the time when I supervised interns in the parent-infant program where Dr. Tom Forrest and I introduced an approach to caregiving that has been variously referred to as the Pikler, the Gerber, the Demonstration Infant Program (DIP), and the Resources for Infant Educarers (RIE) approach. This approach, based on the work of Dr. Emmi Pikler of Hungary, stresses the importance of respectful, responsive, and reciprocal adult-infant interaction. One day, after an intern and I had visited a mother and her six-month-old baby, we discussed the observable differences in the way this mother related to her baby after participating in a few sessions of our parent-infant group. "If we could improve the care of infants, we could improve the world," said I, modestly. "But how many parents and professional parent substitutes can we reach? We work with small groups of four to six infants and their parents, and it would take 100 years to make an impact."

We believed then and still do that it is necessary for parents to *see* how we communicate with infants because, ideally, experience is the best teacher. We did not trust that writing about it would be effective since further removed from experience is the printed word. We were determined, however, and said, "We'll find a way. We will at least make a dent in the world."

This book is the "dent" we had talked about. It successfully bridges the gap between words and experience, between theory and practice, by helping us translate into action in our daily lives such words as *promoting self-esteem, autonomy,* and *optimal development.* The authors have succeeded in writing a practical and personal book, with exercises that help readers develop insights into their own values, behaviors, attitudes, and goals. By encouraging us to write down our own thoughts and reactions, this book takes on the character of a personal diary.

From the beginning of Chapter 1, the reader is invited to view an imaginary videotape. Who could not identify with the mother of a fourteen-month-old girl who is tearing an expensive book to pieces? As mother enters the room with two infant care books in her hand and a "frozen understanding smile" on her face, voices bombard her: "Rotten kid"; "Ignore it"; "She's trying to work out her tensions"; "Spank her"; "You never know in what awful ways spanking may warp her." With clever humor the authors refer to this mother's confusion about different professional perspectives as "Analysis Paralysis."

I vividly remember experiencing analysis paralysis as a mother of young children but was led to see and understand infants in a new way by Dr. Pikler, whose approach to caregiving showed me how to put respect for infants into action. If we accept that even the youngest infant can and should be talked to and treated with respect, and if we are aware of how often we may treat infants kindly yet not respectfully (e.g., picking up a baby from behind without warning), we can bring about changes in our attitudes and the behavior of our infants.

With empathy toward parents, and a gentle and sometimes humorous manner, the authors give many examples that provide the reader the opportunity to develop respectful, responsive, and reciprocal interaction with infants. We learn, for example, that infants can come to successfully communicate their needs and wants if adults take the time to really listen to and understand their needs while they are working out a problem. Adults must be supportive and provide the necessary help, without taking over. This kind of interaction promotes mutual respect in both the home and group care situations.

Infancy and Caregiving will appeal to a wide variety of readers. It provides new insights for parents; for caregiving in day care centers, it presents a guiding theory whose implementation has been worked out in everyday detail. This book has been written with sensitivity, empathy, and respect for both the infant and the adult.

Resources for
Infant Educarers

Magda Gerber
Director

PREFACE

We have used this book in manuscript form in the community college classroom for training caregivers in infant centers, and for training home visitors in an infant-parent development program. We have also used it in a number of ways for parent education.

Consequently we believe that a wide variety of people will find it useful: among them, public health nurses, social workers, counselors, parent educators, high school child development teachers, and others who deal with parents and caregivers. Program directors and training coordinators will find it valuable as a guide for staff training. Furthermore the book especially lends itself to training caregivers who work in day care centers, family day care programs, Home Start infant programs, and infant education and stimulation programs, as well as programs for the developmentally disabled.

The philosophy of caregiving that is spelled out in the ten principles of the first chapter and that underlies the rest of the book came from Magda Gerber and Tom Forrest, M.D., codirectors of Resources for Infant Educarers, a nonprofit organization dedicated to providing resources and support to parents and professionals in infant care. The philosophy was conceived by Emmi Pikler, M.D., in Hungary, and was developed and refined at the Demonstration Infant Program in Palo Alto, California, from 1972 to 1977.

Be not like the child in all ways, child,
For the child in his impatient curiosity pries open the bud,
And the blossom he so wished to see
Is lost to everyone on earth forever.

Let thyself unfold thyself.
Without manipulation even by thee,
Let the life also unfold itself around thee,
Without manipulation by thyself.

Removing impatience, let thy curiosity
Play lightly over this soft unfolding,
Which is essential to the flower of thyself,
For thyself and thy life and the world are one.

If you will but try this soft unfolding, child,
Then the flowering of thyself will be
Both more than you can possibly imagine,
And all that you have wished and longed to be.

BARRY STEVENS and CARL ROGERS
Person to Person: The Problem of Being Human
Copyright © 1967 by Real People Press.
Reprinted by permission.

PART I

Focus on the Caregiver

CHAPTER 1
Introduction

"Knowing about" is different from "knowing how." Knowing about means learning theory. Knowing how puts theory into action. We purposely organized this book to emphasize action because we know that even people with considerable understanding of infants and children have trouble acting on that understanding unless they have also learned how to apply it. Child development experts have problems raising their own children. New teachers who come straight from studying theory find the nursery school a startlingly different world. Although the knowledge they have gained should breed confidence, it does not always do so.

Analysis paralysis

The caregiver who knows a lot about infants and toddlers may occasionally suffer from "analysis paralysis."[1] Analysis paralysis prevents people from making quick decisions, from stating their feelings clearly, and from taking needed action. A common pattern when analysis paralysis strikes is inaction, then indecision, then overemotional or otherwise inappropriate reaction, followed by more inaction. Take for example an inexperienced caregiver in an infant-toddler center who stands by, watching a toddler throwing sand in the air, unsure whether the child's obvious enjoyment of this new accomplishment is more important than the possibility of getting sand in her eyes. She may hang back, doing nothing for a long time, then hesitantly suggest that the child stop, but do nothing when the child continues. She may say or do nothing until the conflict within grows strong enough to cause another reaction. This time she may laugh and play with the child (though hesitantly), enjoying with her the pleasure of her new discovery, until sand gets in someone's eyes, at which time the caregiver may angrily remind the child that she told her to stop a long time ago.

When adults have analysis paralysis and either cannot react or react inconsistently, infants cannot learn to predict what will happen as the result of their own actions. This learning to predict what effect they have on the world is the primary accomplishment infants must make in early life. Depriving them of this learning has an effect on their development. One of the most drastic results of an adult's extreme inability to act appropriately with a child can be failure to thrive—the infant does not develop at all. Somewhat more often, children are delayed to varying degrees in their development and/or may show emotional disturbances.

More commonly, the effects of analysis paralysis are less severe and only cause discomfort in both child and adult. Because of internal conflicts, adults may put up for a long time with behavior that really bothers them a great deal. When intellect and feelings are in conflict, or when two emotions are in conflict, infants and toddlers can sense it. They then continue with behavior which the adults disapprove of—testing to see what will happen. They get no clear message about the proper way to behave, or about the effects of their behavior.

We want to show you an example of a young parent with a case of analysis paralysis to illustrate the points we have mentioned. We appeal to your ability to visualize by presenting an imaginary videotape.

The title appears on the screen (the back of your eyelids). It says in bold letters:

HELP! I'VE GOT ANALYSIS PARALYSIS!

The title dissolves and the camera focuses on a close-up of torn and crumpled paper. We move away as the camera pans the floor of a comfortable family room, then follows a path of paper scraps out the door, down the hall, and into the master bedroom. The path leads to a fourteen-month-old girl who is sitting in the ruins of a very expensive book. The expression on the child's face makes it obvious that she is in the middle of what she knows is a "no-no." Enter mother. She has in her hand two books. We glimpse the word "infant" in the titles. She stops dead in her tracks. On her face is frozen an "understanding" smile. The volume of the sound track swells, and the face dissolves into a scene in which several people are talking. We hear a number of voices. As they begin to separate and become clearer we can distinguish a reasonable, collected adult voice, a quiet, tense, extremely emotional voice, and a harsh scolding voice. Several other voices make a low hum in the background. The babble begins to subside and we can hear the argument.

First voice: (Very low, hard-to-hear gargling sounds expressing speechless fury.)

Second voice: (Reasonable, well-modulated tone.) The child obviously needs to express some inner tension.

First voice: (Low and hard to hear.) Rotten kid!

Second voice: Name-calling destroys self-esteem. Do you want her to identify herself as a rotten kid? She'll have to live up to her name. Let her express herself—it's only a book!

First voice: (Mumbling.) I'm furious! That was my favorite book. I hate that kid.

Second voice: (Pleasantly.) She's only a child trying to work out her tensions.

Third voice: Tensions—smensions! She did that because she's learned to do it. Human beings operate under certain scientific principles. She exhibits behavior for which she is rewarded. Don't give her any social reinforcement for this action. Erase your silly smile, and ignore this behavior.

Second voice: Ignore it! Never! This behavior is a very important indicator of a deeper problem.

Fourth voice: (Harsh and scolding.) Dummy! It's your own fault that this happened. You never should have left that book where she could get it. Don't punish her—punish yourself.

First voice: (Low and whiny.) I can't keep *everything* out of her way. It isn't my fault.

Fifth voice: (Loud and deep.) Spank her! She'll never learn to respect the property of others if you don't spank her!

Second voice: Spank her! And destroy her initiative? At this age she needs to explore, manipulate objects, see herself in control of her environment.

First voice: Oh, be quiet!

Third voice: Rewarding desirable behavior is more effective than punishing undesirable behavior. Punishments leave side effects that one may not be aware of.

Second voice: You want to add to her problems by hurting her? You never know in what awful ways spanking will warp her.

The argument fades. The camera moves back from the group, and again we see the mother's vaguely smiling frozen face. Then we hear a shuffling sound, and the camera moves from her still figure to the child, who is crawling away through the crumpled pages on the floor. We follow the little girl's progress down the hall and into the kitchen. Here she pulls herself up to a table, clutching at a box of crackers. With some effort she gets it down, then delightedly pulls the crackers out of the wrapper one by one and steps on them, lighting up at the crunching sounds they make!

This mother certainly had a case of analysis paralysis. She could give no clear message to her child. Her inaction and frozen smile left the child to try to interpret what she saw in connection with what she must have perceived coming from her mother at the emotional level. We don't know how much destruction it took on the part of the child to get some action out of her mother and to get her mother to outwardly express some feelings. Probably it took plenty of destruction, and when the action did come it was probably bigger than called for in relation to the final incident that provoked it.

We will use "videotapes" like this one throughout the book, to show what we're talking about through examples.

How to use this book

This book is designed not only to be practical, it is designed to be very personal. That is why we chose a workbook format, and that is why this is not an ordinary workbook. Instead of questions that have right or wrong answers, we've designed exercises that lead readers to insights into their own values, behaviors, attitudes, and goals. Sometimes we ask you to write about your own experiences, and we provide exercises that will help you understand the experiences of infants in similar situations. Other times we ask you to add your own suggestions and analyses to those we have presented.

Our method, and the reason for the workbook format, is based on the idea that by talking to yourself through writing, you can become more self-aware.[2] Self-awareness is a vital qualification for caregiving or perhaps for deciding that infant care is not for you. Self-aware people are more likely to be sensitive to the needs of others, which is important when responding to a child too young to express its needs in words. Self-aware people are also more likely to make emotionally honest responses to infants, which is important if infants are to learn to make emotionally honest responses to themselves. And self-aware people are more likely to understand how their behavior is affected by their prejudices, perspectives, and values, and to be less often influenced inappropriately.

Focusing on insights, attitudes, goals, and personal experience through the writing exercises is a preliminary step to acting. We can sometimes avoid analysis paralysis or inconsistent and dishonest reactions (such as those shown on the videotape) by knowing what is happening inside ourselves. The first three exercises, which follow, were designed to help you examine your own attitudes and goals.

Although there are no right or wrong answers to any of the exercises, and they can't be "corrected," it is sometimes helpful to share what you have written with someone else. Our attitudes, values, and opinions often change when exposed to the experiences and ideas of others. So we suggest that when this book is used in a classroom or workshop some arrangement be made to share what is written (though no one should be forced to share anything that he or she considers too personal).

React in writing to the following phrases by putting down the first thing that comes to your mind.

Infants are . . .

Infants need . . .

What I remember about being an infant is . . .

I get turned on by infants when they . . .

I get turned off by infants when they . . .

What worries me most about relating to infants is . . .

Infants should . . .

Parents should . . .

Now look over your reactions. Which attitudes do you feel are individual? Which do you feel are cultural? Are there any you would like to change? How does what you have written show your values? Write about your attitudes and values here.

You can decide how to act as a parent or caregiver for young children only if you have given some thought to what it is that you are trying to do. What are you aiming for? What is your ideal? What are your goals? The following exercise is designed to help you clarify your goals. It takes some time and some materials.

Start by gathering some old magazines, a piece of paper or cardboard, a pair of scissors, and glue. Go through the magazines and find pictures and/or words that say something about the goal you have in mind for child raising, caregiving, or teaching. Some questions to ask yourself as you work are: What do I hope will be the outcome of my caregiving? What kind of child am I trying to raise or teach? What kind of adult do I hope that child might become? Am I that kind of adult? What do I hope will happen as a result of my caring for infants?

Now, using pictures, symbols, or words that say something to you, cut them out and make a collage. When you are finished, put into a few words of your own (a sentence or a poem) what your collage says to you. Write them here.

By now you should have an image and a written summary of your goals as well as some insights into your attitudes and values. As you work through this book, keep in mind the words you have written to summarize your goals. It is important that you be aware of whether or not your actions in dealing with the infants and toddlers in your care are likely to bring you closer to your goals for yourself and for them (and to the parents' goals as well).

The best word for our chief goal as teachers and caregivers is *respect*. We believe that it is vital to raise infants and toddlers to become people who respect themselves and others. And we believe that we can do that by respecting *them* at all times. The question "How do you treat an infant with respect?" pervades the book. Part of the answer lies in every chapter. We'll start to answer it now by giving you the principles on which this book is based—the principles of relating to an infant or toddler with respect.[3]

1. Do involve infants in things that concern them.
   Don't work around them or distract them to get the job done faster.

2. Do invest in quality time, when you are totally available to the infant.
   Don't settle for being always together but only "half there."

3. Do learn infants' unique ways of communicating (cries, words, movements, gestures, facial expressions, body positions) and teach them yours.

   Don't underestimate their ability to communicate.

4. Do invest in time and energy to build a total person.

   Don't strive just to "make the baby smart."

5. Do respect infants as individuals.

   Don't treat them as cute, empty-headed dolls to be manipulated.

6. Do be honest about your feelings.

   Don't pretend to feel something that you don't or not to feel something that you do.

7. Do model the behavior you want to teach.

   Don't preach.

8. Do let infants learn to solve their own problems.

   Don't take away valuable learning opportunities.

9. Do build security by teaching trust.

   Don't teach distrust by being undependable.

10. Do be concerned about the quality of development in each stage.

    Don't rush infants to reach developmental milestones.

These principles will be shown in action throughout the book, especially in Part I. They are supported by the information on infant development in Part II. Chapter 2 examines the special relationship that can grow between infants and adults during caregiving. Chapter 3 describes basic caregiving tasks, and shows how the caregiver can promote the infant's development, as well as teaching self-help skills, while carrying them out. Chapter 4 defines infant education and suggests ways of facilitating infants' development. Chapter 5 shows how the principles of caregiving are related to an infant center curriculum. Chapter 6 shows the importance of attachment and suggests ways of promoting it. Chapters 7 and 8 discuss the development of the sensory and motor systems, perception, intelligence, and language. Chapter 9 examines the emotions of infants and ends with a discussion of the development of a sense of self.

The appendix is a chart showing levels of development, the caregiver's role at each level, and appropriate physical environments (including toys and equipment). This is meant to be a quick, practical reference or guide on setting up an infant care center to promote physical, emotional, social, intellectual, and language development.

Some definitions

Before we begin to examine the principles of caregiving we should explain our terms. We have used the general word "baby" to mean children from birth to approximately three years, which is the age span this book deals with. We have used "infants" to mean babies from birth until they learn to walk, and "toddlers" for babies from the time they walk until they are nearly three. However, the term "infant center" is used in a broader sense to mean a center that serves both infants and toddlers.

We chose the word "caregiver" to label the adult who works in an infant center or family day care home. Other words used to describe this same person are teacher, carer, aide, and "educarer," a word coined by Magda Gerber and Tom Forrest at the Demonstration Infant Program. Although we have chosen "caregiver" because it describes the most obvious function of the job, we use it also to mean teacher and educator.

The term "infant education" is used to mean facilitating development in all areas. Since education is often thought of as dealing only with the intellect, we want to make it clear that our use of the word "education" has a broader meaning.

Notes

1 So far as we know the expression "analysis paralysis" was first used by Lilian Katz, Professor of Early Childhood Education at the University of Illinois, Urbana, Illinois.

2 Although our method is not the same as Ira Progoff's, we developed it from the intensive journal process that he devised.

3 These principles came from one author's experience at the Demonstration Infant Program of the Children's Health Council, Palo Alto, California, directed by Magda Gerber and Tom Forrest, M.D. The philosophy on which they are based was conceived by Emmi Pikler, M.D., in Hungary and was developed and refined at the Demonstration Infant Program.

CHAPTER 2
Principles of
Caregiving

his book is about relationships—the relationships of caregivers and babies. In Chapter 1 we listed ten principles for building the kind of adult-infant relationship that promotes mutual respect. In this chapter we will examine those principles more closely. We'll start by discussing the relationship they are designed to promote.

The relationship we are talking about is one that is respectful, responsive, and reciprocal.[1] It exhibits the give-and-take that indicates a partnership or team, in which the actions of one partner call forth the response of the other, in a kind of chain reaction. Such a relationship is built on a series of respectful, responsive and reciprocal interactions. The following scene shows the type of interaction that builds a good relationship between an adult and an infant.

The scene opens with a five-month-old lying on the floor with several toys scattered within reach. The infant is with six other infants and toddlers in the room. She is contentedly surveying the others as they move around. Reaching now and then, she caresses a toy first with her eyes, then with her hands. As we look more closely, we can see that some suspicious moisture has crept onto the infant's outer clothes in the area of her bottom. We are seeing a very contented, but a very wet, young person. A step is heard offstage, and the infant's eyes travel in the direction of the sound. Then we see a pair of legs and feet traveling along in the direction of the infant. A voice says:

Voice: Jennifer, I'm wondering how you're getting along.

The legs move over close to the blanket and the rest of the person appears. We see a kindly face come close. We catch the caregiver and infant locked in a mutual look. Jennifer smiles and makes a cooing noise. The caregiver responds, then notices the dampness of the clothing.

Caregiver: Oh, Jennifer, you need a change.
Jennifer: (Smiles and coos.)
Caregiver: I'm going to pick you up now. (Reaches out.)
Jennifer: (Responds ever so slightly, continuing to smile and coo.)
Caregiver: (Carries her to a changing table in the corner of the room.)
Jennifer: (Reaches for a toy as she goes by the toy shelves.)
Caregiver: Yes, you can play with that in a minute. I know you want it, but first I'm going to change your diapers.
Jennifer: (Lies on the changing table, but looks elsewhere.)
Caregiver: (Removes the pins in the diaper.) Look, Jennifer, I'm taking out the pins. (Shows them to Jennifer.)
Jennifer: (Starts to squirm and fuss a bit.)
Caregiver: Now I'm taking off the wet diaper. See how wet it is, Jennifer. I'll put it in the bucket. (Disposes of diaper.)
Jennifer: (Squirms to watch.)
Caregiver: Now the powder. See the powder box, Jen.
Jennifer: (Gets distracted—then comes back to touch the powder box.)
Caregiver: Now I'm going to put the powder on.
Jennifer: (Gets distracted by a loud noise in the room.)
Caregiver: (Waits. Touches her.) Open your legs, Jen.
Jennifer: (Brings her attention back to caregiver.)
Caregiver: (Puts the powder on.) Now, here's the clean diaper. Feel the clean one, Jen. (Hands it to her.)
Jennifer: (Reaches for the diaper just as a voice calls the caregiver.)
Voice: Susan! I fixed it! Come look!
Caregiver: I can't come right now, Greg. I'm changing Jennifer. I'll be with you when I'm finished. (Turns back to Jennifer and gives her the diaper.)
Jennifer: (Puts the diaper on her face, pulls it off, laughs.)
Caregiver: (Responds, enjoying Jennifer's pleasure.)
Jennifer: (Begins to squirm and tries to roll over.)

Caregiver: We're not finished yet. Here's where the diaper goes—right on
   your bottom. (Pats her bottom and brings her back to the task.) Now for
   the pins.
Jennifer: (Twists to watch the caregiver put the pins in.)
Caregiver: (Smiles at her efforts.) That's right, Jennifer. I put the pins in like
   this.
Jennifer: (Starts to squirm again.)
Caregiver: Almost finished. Just the snaps left.
Jennifer: (Twists again to watch the caregiver fasten the snaps.)
Caregiver: That's it—we're finished. (Reaches to pick her up.) Want to come
   up?
Jennifer: (Reaches out and sticks her fingers in her caregiver's mouth.)
Caregiver: (Blows on her fingers.) BRRRRR. (Smiles.)
Jennifer: (Smiles back.)

The caregiver picks Jennifer up in her arms and gives her a hug.

   This scene illustrates a responsive interaction chain, as well as five of the ten
principles, though the activity was nothing more than diapering. We'll now
consider each of the ten principles of adult-infant interaction in detail.

Principle 1: Involve infants in things that concern them.

Look at the above scene in terms of the first principle. How many times the
opportunity for distraction occurred! It would have been easy for the caregiver to
give Jennifer a toy to play with, to distract her by talking about other things, to turn
on a music box, or to call upon another child to entertain her. Yet the caregiver's
primary goal was to keep Jennifer interested in the task at hand. To involve her in
what was going on was to get her to pay attention. A spirit of teamwork can come
from a number of situations like this over a long period of time. Jennifer doesn't
just have things done to her. She and her caregiver do them together. These
situations aren't exotic, hard-to-set-up "educational experiences." They are
common, everyday events. From experiences like these, Jennifer gets an education in human relations from which she can build her whole outlook toward life
and people.

   There is a rumor that infants and toddlers have short attention spans. They can't
pay attention to anything for very long, we are told. You can test that rumor for
yourself. Watch an infant or toddler who is actually involved in something that
concerns and interests him. Clock the amount of time he spends on the task or
event. You may be surprised at what a long attention span infants and toddlers
have when they are interested because they are involved. Consider how long
Jennifer paid attention to her diapering because she was involved in the task.

*Think about a situation when you were involved in a respectful, reciprocal
interaction. Write about it here:*

How did writing about that situation help you further understand the first principle?

Principle 2: Invest in quality time.

The videotape of Jennifer and her caregiver was a good example of one kind of quality time. The caregiver was fully present. That is, she was attending to what was going on; her thoughts were not somewhere else. How often caregiving tasks are done routinely, with neither caregiver nor infant present any way but physically! This caregiver was quite conscious of quality time, as is evident by the way she handled Greg's interruption. How much more efficient it would have been to deal with him at the same time she was changing the baby. Obviously it's easy to diaper and talk to someone else at the same time. Yet she valued the time together with Jennifer and apparently had taught Greg about its value. He was probably so willing to leave her alone and wait his turn only because he had experienced quality time himself. Otherwise he might well have continued to try for her attention. He perhaps knew that when she finished with Jennifer, then he might have some minutes of quality time himself.

There are several kinds of quality time. We saw Jennifer and her caregiver sharing quality time because of a task the caregiver had set up. That is one kind. Another kind is when a caregiver makes himself or herself available without directing the action, for instance, just sitting near the baby, fully available and responsive but not in charge. Just being with an infant, passive rather than active, responding rather than initiating, describes this type of quality time. Many psychotherapists attest to the benefits of being fully present to another person without being directive, yet we seldom do it. How many of us receive quality time of that sort ourselves? Think for a moment of the delight of having someone's whole attention at your command.

When was the last time you had someone's full attention for more than two minutes? Write about that here. Did what you experience relate to Principle 2?

Another kind of quality time, perhaps the most commonly understood, is shared activity. This may take the form of playing a game (initiated by either infant or caregiver), reading a story, or spontaneous play involving adult and child.

An interesting aspect of quality time is that a little goes a long way. No one wants (or can stand) intense interaction all the time. Both parties must learn to be private as well. Space and time to be alone are as important for infants and toddlers as for adults. When this time alone never occurs, people try to be private by drifting off, by not paying attention, by being elsewhere mentally if not physically. This attitude becomes a habit, so that time spent constantly together tends to become time when you are only "half there." However, a great deal of "half-there" time doesn't equal even a small amount of "all-there" time.

Of course every infant's life is filled with time that is neither quality time nor private time. The infant has to learn to live in a busy world of people. He is bound to get ignored, moved from place to place, or worked around sometimes. The point is that there is a difference between quality time and other kinds of time, and that all babies deserve and need *some* quality time in their lives.

Ideally the caregiver builds quality time into the daily routine. Diapering, dressing, and feeding are natural occasions for close one-to-one interactions. In a day care center, where a caregiver is responsible for several babies, this becomes more difficult. Some provision must be made so that a caregiver can be freed from watching more children than the one she is diapering or feeding. That means that while one caregiver is giving quality time, the other caregivers may be giving undirected supervision to a number of children. If these children also experience quality time during the day, for instance when they are fed and diapered, they will probably respond to the undirected supervision by playing and by demanding little adult attention. Undirected quality time can also occur when enough staff people are available that a caregiver can concentrate wholly on one or two infants during their undirected play, responding to them alone.

Principle 3: Learn infants' unique ways of communicating and teach them yours.

Look at the same videotape in terms of communication. Notice how communication worked. If you reread the script, you will see that the infant Jennifer used her body and her voice to communicate, and that the caregiver responded by interpreting, answering, and discussing. The caregiver did not carry on endless chatter. She said little, but what she said carried a lot of meaning, which she conveyed by her actions as well as her words. She is teaching the child to listen, not to tune out. She is teaching that talking is communication, not distraction. She is teaching words and language, in context, by talking naturally, not repeating words over and over or using baby talk. She also communicated with her body and with sounds other than words—and she responded to the baby's communication (sounds, facial expressions, and body movements).

Think about someone you know rather well. In what way does that person communicate with you without using words? (Think about body language, facial expressions, sounds, movements, actions, etc.) List the ways and what they mean.

You've just listed examples of someone's unique system of communication as a way of illustrating what we mean by this principle.

Eventually babies come to depend more on words to express themselves and less on the other means of communication. They learn to express needs, wants, ideas, and feelings more and more clearly. They also learn to enjoy language for itself—to play with words, phrases, and sounds. Adult reactions and encouragement to use language facilitate their development.

Principle 4: Invest in time and energy to build a total person.

An infant is a whole human being—not just a mind with a body to carry it around. Some people worry a good deal about making infants bright. They invest in gadgets that they hope will raise the IQ. The makers of these gadgets know how to advertise. They know that nobody wants a "dull" child. So parents and programs spend money on educational toys and feel they are doing the best for the child.

We believe that no gadget in the world can do much for raising the intelligence level. Intelligence is affected by genetics and by day-to-day experiences. *People* are a vital part of those experiences. An example of one kind of experience that promotes the development of intelligence was seen in the videotape. That experience involved people, not gadgets. Think about the learning that can come from such simple but ongoing exchanges. Compare an experience such as the diapering of Jennifer with being entertained by a mobile that hangs over the changing table. It is much better for the baby to be actively involved in the diapering than to watch a suspended gadget, no matter how attractive.

Principle 5: Respect infants as individuals.

The scene with Jennifer showed an adult acting respectfully toward an infant. We saw the caregiver explaining what was going to happen before it happened. She didn't just pick up the infant and carry her around like an object. She told her first, just as she would have told a helpless adult if it had been necessary to pick up that person and move her to another location. Think for a moment about how a respectful nurse might move a helpless or nearly helpless adult patient from a bed to a wheelchair. The respectful way one adult treats another is the way an adult should treat an infant.

To further understand the concept of respect for young children, try this: Pretend you are working in an infant center when a toddler close by you falls down. How could you respond to him with the same kind of respect that you would show an adult who fell off a ladder? Write about that here.

No one would rush over and pick up a fallen adult without talking to him first. It would be important to find out if he wanted to be helped, comforted, or just left alone, depending on whether he was hurt, upset, or embarrassed. Did you find out first what the toddler needed before you responded to him?

Some more aspects of respect come out in the next scene.

The scene opens with a 12-month-old sitting on the grass eating a piece of banana. He is obviously enjoying the experience in more ways than one. He has squashed the banana in his hand, crammed it in his mouth, and it is now oozing out between his teeth. He is relishing it. He reaches for his mouth with the very last piece and, plop, it falls on the ground. He reaches for it. At that moment, from nowhere appear two dogs who race by between the mother, who is sitting nearby, and the baby. When the dogs are gone, both mother and baby look at the spot where the banana was. It's gone! The baby's eyes open wide, his mouth drops open, and a sorrowful wail comes forth.

Mother: (Picks up baby briskly.) Stop that, Brian. That's nothing to cry about. Don't be silly. That was the last piece anyway.
Brian: (Reacts by changing from sorrow to anger, and his screams become loud and piercing.)
Mother: (Turns to her friend, who is sitting nearby.) This child is so spoiled. I'm going to have to do something about it.
Brian: (Begins to kick along with his screams.)
Mother: Stop that now, young man. I'm just about to give you something to really get mad about.
Brian: (Continues to cry, though he has begun to let up a bit.)
Mother: (To her friend.) I've had about all I can take of this. I think he needs a nap. He's touchy when he's tired. (All this said without regard to Brian's presence.)
Friend: (Goes to Brian and hugs him sympathetically.) Poor little sweetheart.
Mother: Well, he has to learn about these things. I think we'd better go on home now. Let's get together again soon. (Picks Brian up without a word and puts him, crying, into his stroller.)

As they leave we watch them go down the path. The two figures are finally gone, and only the crying remains in the air.

What did that scene have to do with respect? Now watch another version of that same scene.

The scene opens the same way. We watch Brian relish his last piece of banana, drop it, and lose it forever as the two dogs race by. As Brian starts to wail, his mother leans over, puts a hand on his shoulder, and says calmly,

Mother: You lost your banana.
Brian: (Pauses for a moment, looks at her, then when the full impact of the experience hits him, he begins to scream.)
Mother: I don't know if you're angry about the banana or scared because of the dogs.
Brian: (Begins to kick, and his screams become more and more piercing.)

Mother: I guess you're mad because you lost your banana. (Her voice still calm.)

Brian: (Continues to cry but not quite so loudly.)

Mother: It's okay to be mad. You lost your banana and you don't like that.

Brian: (Continues to cry.)

Mother: (Waits beside him.)

Brian: (Still sobbing, crawls over to her lap and buries his head.)

Mother: (Pats him gently. Waits. After some time looks at her friend.) Do you know what time it is?

Friend: About 1:30.

Mother: I didn't know it was that late. I guess we'd better be going. Brian . . .

Brian: (Looks at mother and friend. Occasional sobs issue forth.)

Mother: We need to go now, Brian.

Brian: (Looks toward his stroller.)

Mother: Come on.

Brian: (Gets up and crawls toward stroller.)

As the scene ends we see the friends saying goodbye. Brian has become absorbed in the blobs of banana left on his fingers and is licking them as the pair start down the path. The figures disappear on the path and the last sound left in the air is one final gasp of a sob.

There is quite a contrast between these two scenes. In the second one the mother respected the child's right to have feelings and to express them. She offered support without giving sympathy. Perhaps that seems strange, or hard to do. But what you saw was a child who was able to pay attention to what was going on inside himself as a result of the way his mother reacted to the situation. He wasn't distracted by getting his mother's warm, sympathetic feelings superimposed on his anger. In other words he was learning to respond honestly to the situation. If she had stepped in immediately with comfort and hugs (to "make it all better") he might associate the warm attention with the anger. He might learn that anger (or suffering) brings rewards. That kind of learning separates the emotion from the event. In time, the child might learn to use anger to elicit warm feelings when he wants them rather than learning to directly express his desire for the warm feelings.

Notice that after Brian's anger had cooled off a bit, he could then show his mother that he needed and wanted her warmth. She was available when he indicated that he needed her, and he didn't hesitate to crawl over to her lap. She waited for him to indicate what he wanted or needed rather than picking him up immediately. Notice, too, that she stayed in the situation with her son rather than starting to talk about him in front of him to her friend. This last point is a simple one, but one often ignored. When you talk about someone in front of him as if he didn't exist, the message you give is that he is an object rather than a person. If you must talk to a third person about a baby, include the baby in the conversation in some way.

Principle 6: Be honest about your feelings.

In the last scene the child was encouraged to recognize his feelings. He was angry and he was not asked to pretend to be something else. What about adults? There have been no frustrated, unhappy, or angry adults in the videotapes so far. Let's take a look at how one expresses honest angry feelings.

We see a mother flying around a bedroom gathering objects and stuffing them hurriedly in a diaper bag. She glances toward the living room calling, "I'm almost ready!" A little girl crawls back and forth trying to keep out of her way, yet continually getting under her feet. The child is all dressed up and spotlessly clean. The mother pauses in her flurry to comb the child's hair, worrying over each curl. Then she goes back to her packing chores. The baby quietly disappears from the room. Several more times the mother glances toward the other room and reassures whoever is waiting that she won't be much longer. Finally she fastens the last snap on the diaper bag, pats her hair in the mirror, takes a deep breath, and announces, "At last, we're ready to go!" At that very moment we hear a strange splashing sound. Mother turns into the hall and sees, emerging from the bathroom, a soaking wet child, who has just crawled through a puddle of water that was once in a diaper bucket. The mother's face is a picture of strong emotion, and she lets out little gasps. The dripping baby crawls to her feet, slaps her on the leg, and starts to giggle.

Mother: I know you don't understand this, but I'm furious right now, Susan. We're late and now you're all wet!

Susan: (Crawls back toward the dumped diaper pail to play with its contents.)

Mother: (Removes her from her play.) I don't want you to play in the diaper pail.

Susan: (Looks up at her mother questioningly. Starts back for the pail, grinning.)

Mother: I'm too mad to talk to you right now, Susan. (Goes into the bathroom and shuts the door.)

Here was a mother saying honestly what effect the baby's actions had on her. Notice how she expressed her feelings. She didn't put on such a show as to hook the baby on doing it again for her own entertainment. She didn't blame, accuse, judge, or belittle Susan. She verbalized her feelings and connected them clearly to the situation. She let Susan know what made her angry and stopped her from continuing the action. Having expressed herself, she left the scene. In short, she neither masked her feelings nor blew up.

Compare this reaction to the times you've seen people angry with a child, yet smiling and talking in a honeyed voice. Imagine the difficulty a child has in reconciling the two sets of messages that he gets at the same time.

Principle 7: Model the behavior you want to teach.

Already you have seen caregivers modeling the behavior that they hope to teach, with the exception of the disrespectful mother in the park. You've seen them modeling cooperation, respect, honest feelings, and communication. Let's see how this principle works in a possibly more difficult situation, when aggression is involved.

The scene opens on a close-up of a rag doll. She has a sad expression on her face, and as the camera moves back we see that the expression is appropriate, because she is the object of a tug-of-war between two 16-month-old boys. Her arms are stretched almost to the point of tearing, when one boy reaches out and slaps the other. A wail goes up and a caregiver quickly appears. He kneels down beside the two children. His face is calm, his movements are slow and careful. He reaches out and touches the child who did the hitting.

Caregiver: Gently Kim, gently. (Rubs his arm in the same spot where the other child was hit.)

Kim: (Looks angry but remains silent.)

Caregiver: (Turns to the child who was hit. Touches him gently on the same spot.) You got hit, didn't you, Carl. It hurt!

Carl: (Stops crying in response to the touch and soothing voice.)

Caregiver: (Remains quietly, waiting to see what will happen next.) You both want the same doll.

Carl: (Clutches the doll and starts away with it.)

Kim: (Reaches out and grabs the doll.)

Caregiver: (Remains at the scene but doesn't interfere.)

Kim: (Reaches out to hit again, but the caregiver stops his arm in mid-air, gently.)

Caregiver: Gently, gently, Kim. (Touches him softly.) I can't let you hurt Carl.

Kim: (Jerks the doll, and Carl lets go unexpectedly. Takes the doll in triumph and starts across the room.)

Carl: (Looks sad but remains in the same spot.)

Caregiver: (Stays near but doesn't say anything.)

Kim: (Sees a ball on the other side of the room. He drops the doll and goes after the ball.)

Carl: (Comes up quietly and takes the doll, holds her in his arms and coos at her.)

The scene ends with both children playing contentedly and the caregiver no longer needed.

Notice how this caregiver modeled gentleness—the behavior he wished to teach. Consider how often in such a situation the adult arrives on the scene of a dispute and treats the children with more aggression than they have been display-ing themselves. "Don't hit!" says the adult (whack!). "I'll teach you to hit!" (spank, spank, spank). Children learn more from what we do than from what we say. The longest speech on gentleness won't do the same job as the real-life display of gentleness.

The very common situation in this scene is more complex than it may seem. Both aggressor and victim are fearful and need assurance that control will be provided when it is needed. The aggressor needs to be dealt with gently and nonjudgmentally. The victim needs to be dealt with empathetically but not sympathetically (that is, acknowledging his distress without feeling sorry for him). Sympathy may reward the victim for being a victim. How sad that some children *learn* to be a victim because being victimized pays off in love and attention.

Principle 8: Let infants learn to solve their own problems.

The same scene also illustrates this principle: let children (even babies) handle their own problems to the extent that they can. The caregiver could have stepped in and taken care of this situation by creating a solution for the conflict. He didn't, however. He let the infants make a decision themselves. Infants can probably solve more problems than many people give them credit for. The caregiver's role is to give them time and freedom to work on them. That means not responding to every frustration immediately. Sometimes a bit of facilitating will move a child forward when he gets stuck on a problem, but the facilitating should be the least help necessary, leaving the child free to work toward his own solution. Problems are valuable learning opportunities.

Can you remember a time when you weren't allowed to solve a problem that you considered a challenge? Maybe you were working hard trying to do something when someone came along and said, "Here, let me do that for you," and took the problem out of your hands. What was your reaction?

Can you see a parallel between your situation and that of infants who get rescued from most of their problems by well-meaning adults who want to save them frustration?

Principle 9: Build security by teaching trust.

For infants to learn trust, they need dependable adults. All but one of the scenes so far have shown examples of dependable adults who offered strength and support. They didn't trick the baby.

Think what happens when a mother leaves a child by saying good-bye outright. It may be hard to do that when the mother knows the child is going to suffer (probably loudly, with protests and wails), but if the mother (or caregiver) accepts the baby's right to be unhappy and to express it, she will not sneak away. The baby learns to depend on his mother. He comes to know that as long as she hasn't said good-bye, she is still around. He spends far less time and energy worrying about the whereabouts of his mother than the baby who must constantly check to see if she is around, because he never knows when she comes and goes. The baby comes to depend on his knowledge that his mother doesn't lie to him or trick him.

Principle 10: Be concerned about the quality of development in each stage.

Many of us have the idea that faster is better. Some people chart milestones and cheer when their child gets to one early. In the care of people with this attitude, babies are propped up before they can sit on their own, they are walked around by the hand before they can stand by themselves. The important learnings come only when the baby is ready to learn, however, not when the adult is ready to teach.

Each baby is a unique individual who develops in his own way at his own time. Rather than try to push him ahead in his development, caregivers ought to concentrate on broadening his experience in the stage where he is. For instance if he is crawling, celebrate the crawling. The only time in his life he'll ever be so conveniently close to things is the same time in his life when he is so very curious about everything that is within reach and just beyond it. Caregivers can provide experiences and opportunities for him to develop not only his crawling but his curiosity. The question to ask is, not is the baby reaching milestones with great speed, but rather, *how well* does the baby do what it is that he *is doing*?

The ten principles for respectful adult-infant interactions carry with them regard for the individual: the infant is treated as the full human being that he or she is, regardless of age and degree of helplessness. A good adult-infant relationship is built on a series of respectful, responsive, reciprocal interactions over a period of time. Such a relationship is the basis of good caregiving.

As you read the caregiving situations that arise in succeeding chapters, ask yourself the following questions: What would I *probably* do? What effect would my actions be likely to have? What might be a better response? Why? What feelings or circumstances would keep me from doing what I think might be better? And what help do the principles in this chapter provide?

Notes

1 Magda Gerber calls this relationship a "synchronous relationship."

Further reading

Satir, Virginia. *Peoplemaking.* Palo Alto, Ca.: Science and Behavior Books, 1972.

CHAPTER 3
Promoting Development Through Caregiving

Caregiving means responding to helpless or partially helpless people by meeting the needs that they cannot meet themselves. People's most obvious basic needs are the physical ones: food, elimination, cleanliness, warmth, and rest. Caring for infants thus means feeding (including nursing and bottle feeding), diapering, bathing and washing, dressing, and providing appropriate times and circumstances for sleeping. The psychological needs of an infant are less apparent, but also of concern to the caregiver. Some of these needs are met through meeting physical needs alone; others are met by the *manner* in which physical needs are provided for. For example, developing a responsive, respective adult-infant relationship while providing physical care can meet infants' needs for security, power, attention, and closeness, among others. Those psychological needs will be discussed throughout the book, especially in the chapters on attachment and feelings. This chapter focuses mainly on addressing physical needs, but keep in mind, throughout, that they are intertwined with psychological, or emotional, needs.

Determining what an infant needs (especially one who is too young to express himself beyond squirming and crying) is the first step in caregiving. Before you can decide what to do as a caregiver (i.e., which task to perform), you must ask the question, "What is it this baby really needs?" This is a much easier question to ask than it is to answer, especially in the urgency of the moment, when the baby is already screaming. The best approach we can suggest, if the need is not immediately obvious, is to *ask the infant* (yes, even the very youngest one). Ask aloud. Talk to the infant, expressing your desire to understand what he needs. Listen, look, and feel for his answer. If you're beginning to learn his system of communication (the third principle in Chapter 2), you may get your answer directly from him. By taking this approach you're beginning to set up a two-way communication pattern that will serve him well for the rest of his life. Children (even the youngest) who are encouraged to express their needs can become quite skilled at doing just that.

It sometimes—perhaps often—happens that the caregiver's needs interfere with her ability to see the real needs of the baby. Take a look at an example of a baby who needed rest, while his mother needed closeness.

We see a baby sound asleep, apparently quite contented. Into the room creeps his mother. Softly she comes up to the crib. She touches the baby and pats him gently. He stirs in his sleep, but settles back down. She rubs his back and he stirs again—stretches, groans, and moves around. She picks him up gently and hugs him to her, rocking him. As she stands there in the darkened room holding him, a voice comes from the other room, "Are you coming to bed now?" She tiptoes to the door and says quietly, "I'll be there in a minute. Gary needed cuddling."

Why was the mother moved to do something to or for the baby? Who needed cuddling?

It seems that it should be simple to tune in to the baby's real needs and help fulfill them, yet so many complications arise. We've mentioned some above. Another complication is fulfilling a supposed need as a substitute for the real one. For example, when a baby is uncomfortable, restless, sleepy, or irritable, he may be given food. Giving food when the baby needs rest or fondling complicates matters. How is the child to learn later to satisfy his real needs if he learns to take food as a substitute. Will he come to know what is really going on inside himself, or will he automatically reach for a snack when something troubles him?

Some needs cannot be met by caregivers. For example, some infants cannot go to sleep without crying. In those cases the best approach, when you're sure the infant needs sleep, is to put him in his crib, let *him* know that you realize he feels like crying, then accept his crying (that is, don't make yourself responsible for his not ceasing to cry).

In an infant center, just as at home, needs must often be prioritized. Several infants may simultaneously make demands that cannot be met by the number of adults available. Once again the best approach is to let the baby know that his need has been recognized and then accept the fact that he may cry until it is his turn for attention. If you can think of the crying as good—as a sign that he is communicating his needs, it is sometimes easier to accept. When it is his turn, you will of course want to give him your full attention.

Think of a time when you needed something that you could not get by yourself. How did you communicate this need? Were you direct about it? Was your message received? Did you get the results you wanted?

Does anything from this experience relate to fulfilling the needs of infants?

The key to effective caregiving is the good relationship described in the last chapter. Because we believe that the relationship of caregiver to infant is so vital to good caregiving we'd like to give some more attention to describing it. This poetic description by Anne Morrow Lindbergh says a great deal:

> A good relationship has a pattern like a dance and is built on some of the same rules. The partners do not need to hold on tightly, because they move confidently in the same pattern, intricate but gay and swift and free, like a country dance of Mozart's. To touch heavily would be to arrest the pattern and freeze the moment, to check the endlessly changing beauty of its unfolding . . . now arm in arm, now face to face, now back to back—it does not matter which. Because they know they are partners moving to the same rhythm, creating a pattern together and being visibly nourished by it.
>
> The joy of such a pattern is not only the joy of creating or the joy of participating, it is also the joy of living in the moment. Lightness of touch and living in the moment are intertwined. One can't dance well unless one is completely in time with the music, not leaning back to the last step or pressing forward to the next one, but poised directly on the present step as it comes. [1]

Take a look now at an example of a good relationship in one of the primary caregiving tasks—feeding an infant. Imagine yourself in a small body being held lovingly on a warm lap.

> Hear a familiar voice say to you, "Here's some applesauce for you." Look around and see a spoon, a hand, and beyond it a small dish of applesauce. Take time to really perceive all this. Feel the coziness as well as the anticipation. Hear the same voice say, "Are you ready?" See the spoon come up to your face. There is plenty of time for you to open your mouth for the bite. You feel the applesauce in your mouth. You taste it. You notice the texture and the temperature. You thoroughly explore this bite before you swallow. Some goes down your throat, some runs down your chin. You look up to find the familiar face. Seeing the face adds to your pleasure. You open your mouth again. You feel a scraping on your chin. The next bite comes into your mouth. You explore it. You compare it to the first bite. You take your time and get the most out of this bite before you swallow it. When you swallow you get an excited feeling—an anticipation of the next bite. You look at the face again. You reach out and your fingers touch something soft and smooth. All of these feelings are present as you open your mouth for the next bite.

Come back now from your imagining. Reflect on this experience for a moment. Now compare that imaginary experience with this one:

> You find yourself high up in the air. The ground looks very far away. You feel something hard and cold at your back and a strap pushing in to your middle. You are barely able to take in these feelings when suddenly there is a spoon in between your lips forcing them open. You taste applesauce. You wiggle your tongue around swallowing down the bite. The spoon again comes between your lips and your teeth are forced open. You take another mouthful. You enjoy it a great deal—pushing it around in your mouth and out between your

teeth—down your chin. You feel metal scraping your chin. More applesauce comes in to your mouth. You are about to swallow this mouthful when the spoon arrives again. You take a second mouthful into the first, which you haven't swallowed yet. You work on swallowing while you feel scrape, scrape on your chin, as the spoon gathers up what is running down. More applesauce arrives in your mouth. You swallow a little of the big load and you get ready to swallow more, but before you can, the spoon finds its way in between your teeth again. Now your mouth is fuller than before. You sense a bit of urgency to get this down before the next load. You try to hurry, which only slows you down. More applesauce squishes out and runs down your chin. You feel the spoon—scrape, scrape, scrape, and more applesauce comes in to your mouth. Hold on to that feeling now and stop imagining.

Having done this exercise, we assume that you reacted strongly to the second example of caregiving. What do you think the long-run effects of a number of feedings like the second one might be?

What kinds of effects would you expect from a number of feedings like the first one you saw?

Look at the first experience in light of the ten principles of caregiving. Notice that the infant was involved in how the task progressed. The infant and caregiver were sharing quality time—that is, both were paying full attention to each other and the task at hand. They were interacting responsively. The infant was being respected.

Feeding

In our experience, many parents now feel that breast feeding has many advantages over bottle feeding. For that reason it is important for a center to provide for nursing mothers if possible. Many mothers cannot get to the center for feedings, but more and more are finding ways to manage it. The center can encourage breast feeding by making the mother feel welcome and by providing a place for her and her infant to be quiet and comfortable.

Most infants in all-day infant programs are bottle-fed. They deserve the same kind of one-to-one attention and physical closeness that the breast-fed infant receives. A well-organized center will find ways to release a caregiver to sit and feed an infant while holding him, without requiring that the caregiver jump up and down to take care of the needs of other children. Feeding time should be quality time. One reason is that during feeding, attachments are formed between caregivers and the children they feed. For this reason the same caregiver should feed the same babies daily insofar as possible.

Feeding time does not always go well, even when the caregiver tries hard, especially once children eat solid foods and begin to feed themselves. Eating brings forth a variety of emotions in most people. The adult brings to a feeding situation feelings, ideas, and traditions that have nothing to do with the immediate situation. The adult may bring to the feeding the sum total of all the experiences he or she has had with eating. Discussions of table manners can become as heated as a discussion on religion. People have strong feelings about what should or should not go on at the table. For some people the taboos about what cannot be done are deeply ingrained and very important to them. For others, resentment of the taboos is equally strong. The point is that eating is connected with strong feelings and that these feelings affect the way an adult approaches or reacts to feeding an infant or teaching an infant self-feeding.

We have found that it is much harder to approach feeding with the same patient, sensitive warmth and calm with which other caregiving tasks are approached. As long as things are going well (as in the first experience with the applesauce) it's easy. When things start going wrong, it's a different story. Let's look at an example.

We find ourselves in the kitchen of a family day care home. Several preschoolers are playing with puzzles on the floor. At the sink a tired, tense-looking young man is fixing a bowl of cereal. At a low table watching him is a baby who is alternately fussing and banging on the table with a spoon. The caregiver brings the bowl of cereal and another spoon and sits down on a low chair, bringing himself down to the level of the baby. The baby attacks the cereal with clumsy vigor—slopping it over the side of the bowl and getting only small amounts in his mouth. The caregiver patiently scoops the cereal back into the bowl and helps where he can in the feeding process. He obviously wants the child to do as much for himself as possible. Shortly the baby gets frustrated in his attempts at self-feeding and starts to look toward the man to feed him.

Caregiver: I guess you're still hungry and you want some help. Right?
Baby: (Responds by opening his mouth.)
Caregiver: (Feeds him several spoonfuls in response to his messages.)
Baby: (Looks more satisfied and begins again to put his attention to the spoon in his hand.)
Caregiver: You want to try it now?
Baby: (Continues trying to feed himself.)
Caregiver: There you are! (Looks pleased.)
Baby: (Begins to slow down.)
Caregiver: (Continues to support his efforts without interfering.)
Baby: (Picks up a full spoon of cereal and splats it on the floor, laughing at the sound it makes.)
Caregiver: (Sighs.) Oh, you had an accident. (Leans over to scoop up the mess.)
Baby: (Makes it apparent that he enjoyed his "accident" and is ready to try it again. The minute he has a chance he splats another spoonful.) Giggle, giggle.

Caregiver; Oh, Cleve! (Tensely.)

Baby: (Takes aim with another spoonful.)

Caregiver: I know you're enjoying that, but I'm not. (Takes the spoon and redirects it to his mouth. Cleans up the floor wearily but patiently.)

Baby: (Holds the spoon ready to splat again.)

Caregiver: (Takes his hand.) Cleve! I don't like that!

Baby: (Eats a bite, pauses.)

Caregiver: Maybe you've had enough—is that it?

Baby: (Looks him straight in the eye and picks up a spoonful. Before he can be stopped he splats a spoonful right in the caregiver's face.)

Caregiver: (Reacts with controlled anger. Takes the spoon from his hand, wipes the cereal from his face and looks at the baby firmly.)

Baby: (Looks away and tries to climb out of the chair.)

Caregiver: I get mad when I get hit in the face. I'm going to put the cereal away now. (Takes the bowl and puts it and the spoon on the sink.)

Baby: (Climbs out of his chair and begins to giggle and pull at the pant leg of the caregiver.)

Caregiver: I'm too mad to enjoy you right now. (Leaves him and goes into the other room.)

The scene ends with the baby sitting on the floor looking perplexed as he runs his finger through a dab of cereal he has discovered on the floor.

It's hard to know exactly what feelings were running through this man, though it is obvious that he was getting upset. It was also obvious that Cleve had had his hunger satisfied before his caregiver realized it. Perhaps the caregiver had some conflict about the sensory experience of playing with the food. He seemed willing to let it continue to some extent, yet finally reached the end of his rope. We certainly will not criticize him for the way he expressed and handled his feelings in an honest way. But we will question why he allowed the situation to go on until he reached the point of having such strong feelings. He could have easily ended the meal sooner.

Understanding infants' signals, giving choices, defining limits clearly, reacting honestly, and interacting responsively are all keys to pleasant feeding experiences.

Giving choices is an important part of all aspects of caregiving, and is especially important to feeding. An infant can learn to pay attention to his inner messages if he can make a decision about what to eat. His body asks for what it needs over a period of time. He may not eat a balanced diet every day, but over a period of time he chooses for himself the foods his body needs.[2] Are we suggesting that every meal must be served cafeteria style, with five entrees and six salads to choose from? No. We mean offering a choice of an apple or an orange to the child who is old enough to eat them and then respecting his choice or his refusal. We mean paying attention to how the younger infant responds to what you put in his mouth. In other words, we mean the opposite of forcing, games, and coaxing. When a healthy infant refuses to eat squash or seems to go overboard on cereal, he knows what he is doing.

Here is yet another caregiver in another infant feeding situation.[3] This time we are in an infant center rather than a family day care home.

We focus in on a low table where three seated toddlers are intently watching a man who has several plastic cups in his hand. Across from the man is a woman with an infant in her arms.

Tom: (To the child on his right.) Susan, do you want this cup (holds out a small blue cup without a handle) or this one? (Offers a slightly larger green one with a handle.)

Susan: (Regards both carefully.) Uh . . . (Reaches for the blue one.)

Tom: Now, everyone has a cup. We're ready for the juice. (Brings out a can of apple juice.) See the can of juice. (Takes his time so each child has plenty of chance to realize what is happening. Notices one child is getting particularly excited.) Ricky, you're ready for your juice.

Ricky: (Pounds his cup on the table.) Me! (Reaches cup out to Tom.)

Tom: Yes, you want your juice. We have to open the can first! (Gets out the can opener, taps the top of the can, punctures the lid. Then, still moving slowly, and aware that all eyes are on him, he pours a litle juice into a small pitcher and hands it to Ricky.)

Ricky: (Grabs the pitcher and pours with great excitement, missing his cup.)

Tom: (Hands him a small sponge.) Here's a sponge for the spill.

Ricky: (Pays little attention to the sponge, which finds its way to the spill and lies there sopping up the liquid. Pours again, this time more carefully, the small amount of juice left in the pitcher.) Umm. Me. (Abandons the pitcher and concentrates on the cup.)

Tom: Kim, you're ready for your juice. (Fills the pitcher again and passes it to her.)

Kim: (Takes pitcher, pours some, then shoves the pitcher toward the mother and baby at the table.) Baby want juice too.

Tom: You want Andrea to have some juice. (Watches as the mother pours a small amount of juice into the waiting glass and holds it to her child's lips. An interruption causes everyone's attention to shift to the child at the table who has not yet been served.) Greg, you want to tell us something.

Greg: (Bangs cup, shouting.) Me! Me!

Tom: You want your juice.

Greg: No! Me no juice.

Tom: Maybe you're ready for some fruit. (Gets a small basket with an apple and a banana in it.)

Greg: No!

Tom: You don't want fruit and you don't want juice.

Greg: Me! (Points beyond Tom to the low cupboard containing the food and eating equipment.)

Tom: You want something in the cupboard.

Greg: Me . . . ummm.

Tom: (Notices a jar of raisins in view.) You want some raisins?

Greg: UMMMM. UMMM!

Tom: (Gets the raisins, puts them in a small plastic dish, and offers them to Greg.)

Greg: (Grabs two handfuls and looks delighted.)

Susan: Nanana. Nanana.

Tom: You are ready for some banana. (Brings out the banana for closer inspection by the children.) We have to take off the peel. (Let's each feel the peel.) The banana is inside. (Slowly and with full attention of each child, he pulls off the peel.)

Susan: (Squeals with delight.)

Tom: Are you ready for a piece, Susan? (Offers her a piece of banana.)

Susan: (Takes the banana and squishes it in her fingers. Then with obvious enjoyment licks each finger.)

Ricky: Me! (Takes the bite offered him, stuffs it all in his mouth, and holds out his hand for more.)

Notice that the caregiver was dedicated to the idea that children learn a good deal from examining and exploring the food they eat. Notice how he encouraged each child to touch, smell, notice the food—the form it came in, the way it changed, the parts it was made up of. We saw here a terrific experience in perception and cognition. Notice the contrast between the upset adult in the previous videotape and the peaceful caregiver here. The first man was not sure where to draw the line between a meal and a sensory experience, and he allowed the child to go beyond the point where he, the caregiver, felt comfortable. The second man was comfortable and was convinced that the children were benefitting from the experience. None of the children overstepped this caregiver's limits, but somehow he leaves the impression that he would stop anyone who approached his limits *before* he got angry.

Before we leave the subject of feeding, let's consider some of the equipment that influences the feeding of babies—the high chair and the low table and chair. The advantage of putting babies who can sit alone in low chairs at a low table is that they are not helpless. They can get up and down. They can choose when to do it and not have to call for help. The disadvantage is that they cannot eat as a full member of the family, as they can when they are at table level. Thus the high chair serves a social purpose as well as the caregiver's convenience. For that reason high chairs have probably been used almost without thought on the part of the adults who buy them. However, it is worth considering that in such chairs babies are in a high and possibly precarious-feeling position. They are usually strapped in, which restricts movement, and may be stuck there for a long time since they cannot get in and out without help. Which situation is best depends on the caregiver's priorities.

Diapering

Did you think the diapering episode in Chapter 2 was too idealistic? The following scene is less than ideal, but it is based on the same principles as the first one.

> The scene is a small infant center. The corner of the room is set up for several toddlers who are occupying it right now. One is a small boy playing content- edly with an empty can and a wooden spoon. We see a pair of feet and legs approach. The baby looks up as a voice reaches him.
>
> *Caregiver:* How are you doing, LeRoy? (Sniffs.) Hm. Do I smell something?
> *LeRoy:* (Turns his back.) No!
> *Caregiver:* LeRoy, I think you have a dirty diaper.
> *LeRoy:* No!
> *Caregiver:* I know you don't want to be changed, LeRoy, but I'm going to change you anyway. I'm going to pick you up now. (She holds out her hands.)
> *LeRoy:* (Puts up a fuss.)
> *Caregiver:* (Picks him up firmly, but calmly.)
> *LeRoy:* (Continues to resist.)
> *Caregiver:* You really don't want me to change you.
> *LeRoy:* (Squirms and tries to get away.)
> *Caregiver:* (Holds him firmly.) I'm sorry, but you just have to put up with this. Let's get these pants off. (Waits for the smallest hint of cooperation, which LeRoy reluctantly gives.) There—see the pants are dirty—they go here. (Indicates plastic bag.)
> *LeRoy:* (Looks momentarily at the bag and begins to squirm around in the other direction.)
> *Caregiver:* Now the diapers, LeRoy.
> *LeRoy:* (Pays no attention—squirms and tries to stand up.)
> *Caregiver:* I know you want to stand up, but you have to wait just a minute. See, I'm putting the diaper in the garbage now.
> *LeRoy:* (Ignores her.)
> *Caregiver:* Some water to clean you, LeRoy. (Shows him a wet washcloth.)
> *LeRoy:* (Shows a spark of interest. Turns to where he hears water running.)
> *Caregiver:* Want to touch the water?
> *LeRoy:* No! (Squirms away but looks back as a wet washcloth is presented to him.)
> *Caregiver:* This is the wet washcloth.
> *LeRoy:* (Grabs it—examines it briefly—puts it in his other hand and gets ready to fling it back at his caregiver.)

Caregiver: (Takes cloth gently.) I'm going to clean your bottom.

LeRoy: (Struggles and generally gives his caregiver a bad time.)

Caregiver: (Fastens clean diaper as quickly as she can under the circumstances.) There we go, LeRoy.

LeRoy: (Sees that she is finished and holds up his arms to be taken down.)

Caregiver: Are you ready to get down? (Puts him on the floor.)

LeRoy: (Relaxed and happy now, goes back to playing with the can and wooden spoon as if nothing had happened.)

Although the caregiver in this scene was using the same principles as the first, the diapering was not as easy. All children go through periods of being uncooperative, and it is important that they do so, even though it is hard on the caregiver. Resisting is a sign of growth; by resisting, children assert their individuality. They learn something about the push toward independence that will one day make them individuals who no longer need the kind of care they now receive.

Notice that the caregiver did not give up. She tried to involve the toddler in the task, even though it wasn't easy. She acknowledged his feelings and verbalized them for him. She respected his feeling annoyed and wanting to be active, and worked with as little fuss as she could manage. In short, she treated LeRoy as a human being—never as an object. She treated him with respect.

Can you think of a time in your own life when your push for independence made it hard for others to get along with you? What happened? How were you responded to? What was the result? Does your experience have any relationship to diapering LeRoy? Why or why not?

Bathing

The principles of caregiving apply equally to bathing. For infants the key is to go slowly. Tell them what is happening, and let them anticipate. If babies are told what is happening, are given time to try to comprehend as well as to read the messages from their senses, eventually they will learn to cooperate, because they will come to trust the caregiver as well as the situation. Slow, gentle movements facilitate the process.

Baths for very young infants can be uncomfortable, screaming times. If hurried, the child is more confused and therefore screams more. If the caregiver remains calm and at the same time accepts the infant's fears and feelings, the bath can be a quality experience.

As an infant gets older and is able to sit up in the tub, it is tempting to add toys to the bath water. Toys, however, tend to distract infants from the bathing and to interfere with the adult-child communication; therefore, to aim for teamwork it is probably best to introduce the toys after the actual washing. The more children are allowed to concentrate on the task at hand, the more involved they can become. We do not mean to imply that bath time has to be serious business. As in any caregiving situation, there is room for lighthearted play. Water especially lends itself to play and relaxation.

Dressing

Caregivers can promote autonomy by setting up tasks in such a way that the child makes his maximum contribution. You can easily see examples of this principle in dressing activities. For instance, when taking off the socks or booties of even a very young baby, you can pull them half off and ask the child to finish the job. It takes little coordination, when the task is set up like this. Babies get real pleasure and satisfaction from helping out—even at a young age. The idea is to simplify the task just the right amount so that the child gets practice in the beginnings of the dressing process. At first it takes longer to work cooperatively, but, as infant and caregiver come to see themselves as a team, the earlier patience pays off. Think about how it feels to get the opposite treatment.

> Imagine yourself a young toddler. You are about to be taken outside for a walk with your mother and a neighbor and her baby. The neighbor has arrived and is waiting. Your mother says, "Come here," to you. Before you can respond, you feel your arm being grabbed. You were busy thinking about the baby who has just arrived, and so you were thrown off guard. You feel yourself being hauled over by one arm to where your mother and the neighbor are standing. You hear their voices deep in conversation. You are trying to take in their words and at the same time are concentrating on this baby, who is now quite within reach. You feel your arm being held tight and something comes up over one hand. You barely have time to pull your fingers in. As it is, one thumb gets stuck and stretches back as the sleeve

comes up your arm. You get a bit annoyed, and when you are able to get your thumb back into your fist, you become all floppy. You feel a tighter grip on you and some tension transfers from the hands holding you. You feel even more annoyed. You resist.

You are aware that your mother is busy telling the neighbor all about the difficulties you went through at breakfast time. You relive some of the feelings you went through earlier that day. Finally you feel one arm fully sleeved. Suddenly you feel your whole body spin around. Hands grip your other hand and arm. The other coat sleeve starts up over your hand. You are aware again that you are being talked about, and you try to listen as well as figure out where the sleeve is going. You get floppy again. Finally both arms are in sleeves. You feel a zipper go up—it touches your neck and feels cold, uncomfortable and tight. You look up at your mother, but though her hands are still on the zipper, her face is turned away from you, still talking to the neighbor. You feel a conversation going on right across the top of your head, a conversation still about you. The word "Ready?" goes skimming across the top of your head. Before you have any idea who the word was directed to, you feel yourself being lifted into the air, the door opens, and out you go.

Dressing can be done with respect when the child is treated as a person rather than handled and manipulated as in the scene above. Cooperative dressing leads eventually to the child's taking over the task himself.

Can you remember a time when you were treated as an object rather than as a person? How did you react?

Sleeping

The caregiver's main responsibility in this area lies in determining when the child needs to sleep. In an infant center it is especially important that the child be allowed to rest according to his needs rather than according to a schedule, as in a kindergarten. Some infants take a number of short naps, others take long naps in the morning and short ones in the afternoon, and still others take no morning naps but long afternoon ones. Realize that an infant's sleep pattern needs change— possibly from day to day as well as over a period of time. No one napping schedule will fit all the babies in a center, and each baby's personal schedule changes from time to time. (It may be easier for caregivers in a center to accommodate this need than for parents at home.)

Not all babies express their need for rest in the same way. Experienced, sensitive caregivers learn to read each child's signals, which may range from slowing down and yawning to increased activity and low frustration threshold.

Each baby should have a personal crib that is located in the same spot every day. That kind of consistency and security is needed for easy sleeping. Children who feel nervous, scared, or lacking in trust may have sleep problems that consistency would help alleviate. A favorite toy or blanket may also provide needed security. Sometimes a caregiver can do nothing at the moment to promote security but must acknowledge the insecure feelings of the child and wait until he eventually learns that he is in a safe place.

Decisions about when to put a child in a crib and how long to leave him there when he is not sleeping depend on the adult's perception of the particular child's needs. Some children need to be confined for some time before they can fall asleep, even when they are very tired. They may play or cry before sleeping. Other children fall asleep immediately. The waking up period also takes some adult judgment. Does the child wake up energetic, active and ready to play, or is there a long transition period between sleeping and waking during which the child may need to remain in the crib? Reading a young child's signals about rest needs is not always easy.

Teaching self-help skills

In each of the caregiving areas discussed above, we've mentioned developing self-help skills. Here we will focus more directly on the subject. One of the objectives of caregiving is to work yourself out of a job. That is, a caregiver must gradually teach babies to take care of themselves. This is a long-term task that starts by asking the infants' cooperation. Eventually, step by step, if you take advantage of their readiness, they will take over for themselves. For each baby the time of readiness is different.

We will now look at promoting self-help skills in meeting needs for food, elimination, cleanliness, warmth, and rest.

To teach children to feed themselves start with child-size unbreakable utensils and small amounts of food. It is easier to clean up a little applesauce than a lot. Furthermore babies may feel overwhelmed by a large portion. Finger foods like chunks of fruit further encourage self-help skills and are a welcome treat to the child who is just learning to use utensils. Allow time for play and experimentation, but be aware of your own limits. End the meal for the child before the play begins to bother you. A tension-free setting promotes self-feeding skills.

There is much advice available from many sources about toilet training. We add our own. When a child's dry periods begin to increase, he may be ready to begin toilet training. Other signs of readiness are when he can recognize signals of the need for elimination, can communicate them, and can wait to get to the bathroom. His self toileting will be greatly facilitated by adult models, easy-to-remove clothing, and a low potty chair.

Children can learn to wash their own hands and later their faces if they can reach a sink, soap, and towels. They can also learn to bathe themselves but of course cannot be left alone in the bathtub.

Learning to dress oneself is a skill that takes some time. It starts with getting the infant involved when he is being dressed and undressed. Undressing, of course, is much easier and is learned early by some babies (even when they have not been taught).

Deciding how much clothing is needed is an issue that sometimes produces conflicts between caregivers and infants. Other factors besides warmth enter into the question of whether or not the baby needs a sweater. An infant new to a day care center may not be willing to remove his sweater because it represents security to him. The caregiver must decide whether his physical needs or his psychological needs are more important at the moment.

Helping a child determine his own needs is an important factor to consider concerning rest. Encouraging self-calming behavior from the beginning (thumbsucking is an example) helps a child to begin to take over his own responsibility for rest. Children (and adults) vary in their ability to determine when they need rest and then do something about it.

Except for rest, self-help skills are mainly social skills. Social skills are not naturally present in infants, and they must reach a certain stage of development, a stage of readiness, in order to learn them. The caregiver's role in helping infants acquire social skills is that of *teacher*, in contrast to the subject of the next chapter in which the caregiver's role is primarily that of facilitator.

If adults regard caregiving tasks as vital learning experiences, they are more likely to approach them with patience and attention. In an infant center, even when the staff-to-infant ratio is good, the main opportunity that a baby has to enjoy a long period of one-to-one interaction is during caregiving times like feeding, diapering, and dressing. If those times are used well during the other periods of the baby's day, he requires far less adult attention. The baby can go about his play (interacting with the environment and with the other babies) with no more than general supervision from an adult who may be watching a number of babies.

When infants are treated with respect and caregiving is done with a teamwork approach, they can build relationships as well as learn about themselves and the world. They come to anticipate what will happen to them—that the world has some predictability. They learn that they have some power to influence the world and the people in it. And they begin to make sense out of life. When used to their fullest, these times can become focuses in a child's day—something he looks forward to—his chance to "dance" with his partner!

Notes

1 Anne Morrow Lindbergh, *Gift from the Sea* (New York: Pantheon, 1955), p. 104. Copyright © 1955 by Anne Morrow Lindberg. Reprinted by permission of Pantheon Books, a Division of Random House, Inc.

2 Dr. Clara Davis showed this in 1935 by feeding three infants (eight to ten months old) only foods that they chose to eat. She presented each infant with six to eight dishes all containing wholesome foods. Although the infants did not necessarily choose a balanced diet on any given day, in the long run they did. C. M. Davis, "Self-selection of Food by Children," *The American Journal of Nursing*, 1935, **35**, 403-410.

3 The caregiver is Dr. Tom Forrest at the Demonstration Infant Center. The infants are fictitious.

Further reading

Provence, S. *Guide for the Care of Infants in Groups.* New York: Child Welfare League of America, Inc., 1967.

Willis, A., and Ricciuti, H. *A Good Beginning for Babies: Guidelines for Group Care.* Washington, D.C.: National Association for the Education of Young Children, 1975.

CHAPTER 4
Infant Education

Some infant programs are called "stimulation programs" and are based on the idea that to educate infants is to stimulate them. Our idea of educational programs for infants is *not* based on a stimulation approach for reasons that will become clear below.

Consider the plight of the infant being stimulated:

Imagine an infant lying in a crib in a brightly painted room. She is lying on her back. Directly over her head hangs a mobile that is moving slightly. She looks up at it, but all she sees is the bottom view (the least interesting view of most mobiles). She spends little time looking at it anyway though, because she has already learned that it is out of reach and there is no way she can have any effect on it. She tunes out the mobile. Then she turns instead to a plastic bag of goldfish hanging on the crib. It seems as though she might get interested in this—but as she looks in their direction she sees several pictures on the wall. As she begins to focus on them, music from somewhere cuts into her concentration. She tries to roll over and finds herself in a pile of toys. She feels a variety of textures. She tries to find a blank place to look, a quiet place to be, but there is none. So she puts her thumb in her mouth, whimpers a couple of times, nestles her head into the pile of toys and goes to sleep.

The example is extreme to make a point. Heaping the crib with toys and hanging out-of-reach mobiles do little but give the infant many sensory experiences (in this case too many) in the confined area that is designed for sleeping. In this scene the infant could have no effect on the things around her, except through turning them off by going to sleep. If you are concerned only with stimulating, with doing something *to* the baby, you ignore a vital requirement for learning and development: that babies need to discover that they can influence the people and things around them. Yes, they need stimulation, which they get from objects, and more importantly from people. But they need to perceive their own involvement in these stimulating experiences. Their involvement comes when they are able to have some effect on—that is, interact with—the people and things that are part of the experiences. When stimulation is provided without regard to the baby's response, the baby is being treated as an object.

Facilitating learning

We propose a different approach to infant education. We believe that education results when a baby finds "The 'pleasure of being the cause'—of learning how to act in order to produce the results he wants, of learning about things that are the results of his own actions."[1] Hence we propose a problem-solving approach.

What kinds of problems does an infant face? Watch an infant for just one hour and you will note that he deals with a variety of problems—physical ones, such as hunger or discomfort; manipulative ones, such as how to get a toy from one hand to the other; emotional ones, such as separation from parent or caregiver; and many more. Some problems are specific to his level of development and will eventually be solved. Others are specific to the situation and may or may not be solved. Still others are ones he will be dealing with, in one form or another, throughout his whole lifetime.

Education, we believe, lies in learning to deal with this enormous variety of problems, learning various ways to approach them, and learning when they can be solved and when to give up. As babies continually experience the problems that come from everyday living, the problems they encounter in play as well as in being fed, changed, dressed, bathed, and put to sleep, they eventually come to see themselves as problem solvers. If they come to see themselves as good problem solvers, they will have been well educated, by our definition.

The primary function of the adult in infant education is to facilitate learning rather than to teach or train. Start by appreciating the problems the baby encounters. Allow him to work on solving them himself. Also, you, as caregiver, will present problems to the baby while you provide for his needs and set up the environment for his play. You facilitate infant education by the way you direct and respond to the problem-solving baby.

The role of the adult   We've stated above that the role of the adult is to facilitate the infant's learning. What kind of skills make up the facilitator's role? We will discuss four such skills shortly, but first we will approach the question by examining something that we call "presence."

To understand the idea of "presence," try the following exercise.

The next time you greet someone in an ordinary, polite, perfunctory way, be aware of the experience. ("Hello, how are you?" "Fine, thanks, and you?") Then make a special point of greeting someone by giving your full attention to who they are, what they are saying, what is happening at the moment, how they might be feeling, how you are feeling. Compare the two experiences and think about the implications for relating to infants. Write about these two experiences here.

Notice that in the second greeting you were "fully present," that is, you were giving the person your full attention, concentrating on and responding to the way the other person looked, acted, and possibly felt. Was there a difference in what was said as well as in nonverbal messages sent and received?

Now find someone who is willing to be your mirror.[2] Stand facing that person and ask the person to copy each of your movements. Then using your body, facial expressions, and hands, do something for the "mirror" to copy. You may want to move around. After you have experienced being the doer, try being the mirror.

When you finish, discuss the experience with your partner. What role did you prefer—doing or mirroring (leading or following)? What was hard about each one? What are the advantages and disadvantages of each?

This mirroring exercise shows again the kind of reciprocal interactions that constitute the responsive relationship first discussed in Chapter 1.

In the space below, write about your experience with the exercise and how your preference for one role over the other might affect your relationship with an infant.

There are two ways to give your full attention to an infant in an educational way: *following*, which is receptive and responsive, and *leading*, which is active and directive.

See, in the following videotape, how the adult's being receptive or active works when an infant has a problem to solve.

> *Jason:* (Toddles in crying loudly and holding his fingers out in front of him.)
>
> *Caregiver:* Oh, Jason, something happened to you.
>
> *Jason:* (Continues to cry and holds his fingers up for inspection.)
>
> *Caregiver:* (Touches his fingers gently.) It looks like you hurt your fingers. (Remains very calm.)
>
> *Jason:* (Pulls at caregiver's pants.)
>
> *Caregiver:* You want me to come.
>
> *Jason:* (Moves adult into the other room to a cupboard with the door standing ajar. His cries change to anger.)
>
> *Caregiver:* You pinched your fingers in the door?
>
> *Jason:* (Very angry now. Picks up a toy hammer and gets ready to throw it at the cupboard door.)
>
> *Caregiver:* (Holds his arm.) I know you're mad, but I won't let you throw the hammer. You might hurt something.
>
> *Jason:* (Reconsiders, puts down the hammer and goes to the cupboard. Still crying he closes the door and opens it again. He is very careful in his actions.)
>
> *Caregiver:* Yes, now you can do it without pinching.
>
> *Jason:* (Ignores him and continues to open and close the door. The angry cries subside and a pained whimpering takes their place. He sits down by the cupboard and remains there crying.)
>
> *Caregiver:* (Bends over to him, arms out.) Let's go put some cold water on your fingers.

What we see here is mostly receptive presence. The caregiver followed Jason's lead. Only twice did the caregiver take the lead. Notice that the caregiver was calm and not over emotional, though he was able to empathize with Jason (to feel his hurt). Because he did not get drawn into the situation and could provide support to Jason in his pain, he facilitated Jason's problem-solving abilities. The scene might have been very different if the caregiver had given Jason advice or "taught him a lesson." The scene might also have been very different if the caregiver had offered sympathy. Imagine if he had picked up Jason and murmured supposedly comforting phrases like, "Oh, poor Jason, you got hurt, poor, poor little boy." But the caregiver gave neither advice nor sympathy. Instead he gave his full calm attention, both receptive and active, thereby giving Jason the support, strength, and acceptance he needed to pursue the problem he had encountered.

The adult role of directing and responding to infant problem solving is made up of four skills. The adult must be able to ascertain the optimal level of stress for the infant faced with a problem, provide appropriately for the infant's need for attention, give feedback, and model desired behavior. We will consider each of these skills in turn.

Stress   Stress and frustration are an important part of infant education. They come naturally with problem solving. In order to develop physically, emotionally, and intellectually, the baby occasionally needs something to fight against, to pit his will and strength against. In this way he can discover that he is a competent problem solver. With no stress, no frustrations, and no problems, he has no way to try himself against the world. Consequently his education is severely limited.

A young parent, thinking about stress as a part of infant education, wrote the following:

I was watering my garden the other day and I found out more about stress and development. I'd been watering every day for some time and found that some of my seedlings weren't growing deep roots. As I thought about it—if a plant doesn't have some stress factors so that it has to look for food and water, its roots won't grow as deep, therefore it won't be as stable in the world. Its foundation will be too shallow. [3]

The right amount of stress—not too much, not too little—promotes development. The optimum level of stress depends entirely on the individual. The caregiver must decide what "optimum" means for any particular baby and then try to allow for it—opportunities will arise naturally in daily life.

How can you decide what is enough stress? You can decide the optimum level of stress by watching the infant's actions. Children under too much stress are not able to solve problems effectively; they may become greatly emotional, or they may withdraw. Children who never meet with frustration are not involved in interacting with their environment. You can also decide what is enough stress by being empathetic (imagining what a child is actually feeling) and by remaining calm and not being swayed by either the infant's emotions or your own. Being calm gives a perspective that facilitates good decision making.

What should you do if the infant is either overstressed or understressed? Take a look at the problems the child faces. Perhaps there are too many of them, in which case some changes need to be made to cut down on the number. They may be too hard for him to solve, in which case he may need more help. If the child is understressed, he may not be encountering enough problems in his life—either not enough is happening to him, the environment is lacking in variety or interest, or someone is solving his problems for him.

Can you think of a time in your own life when stress was good for you? Write about that here.

How can you tell the difference between optimal stress and too much stress for yourself? Does this relate to how you can tell when a baby is having too much stress? How?

Attention   The way an adult responds to an infant's actions is an important part of infant education. The adult response has a lot of power, since an infant essentially lives on attention from others, especially the others who are important to him. For each individual there is an optimum amount of attention—optimum again, not maximum. If he gets enough, he'll be satisfied. If he doesn't get enough, he will seek it in a variety of ways.

How do you satisfy your own needs for attention? How aware are you of the ways in which you get people to pay attention to you? Can you list some ways you get attention from other people?

Are you happy with your list? Are you satisfied with the ways in which you meet your needs for attention? Would you want infants to get attention in the same ways?

If a baby finds that smiling, cooing, and being peaceful is not enough, he will try other behaviors. Eventually he will find out how to "push the buttons" of the important people around him. It is important for the adult to recognize when a child is trying to get attention by upsetting him and when he is directly communicating his real needs, but it is not easy to tell the difference. Look at the following situation. What is going on?

We see a mother in the middle of a telephone conversation.

Mother: Hang on a minute, the baby's crying. (Turns from the phone toward the baby on the floor.)

Elisa: (Bangs on the refrigerator door.)

Mother: I'll bet you're thirsty. Okay, just a minute. I'll get you some juice. Just let me finish talking. (Turns back to the phone.)

Elisa: (Screams.)

Mother: (Into the phone.) Just a minute, I have to take care of Elisa. (Puts down the phone, frowns, goes to the refrigerator and pours a little cup of juice, gives it to Elisa at a low table.)

Elisa: (Stops crying. Sits down to drink her juice.)

Mother: (Goes back to the phone, turning her back on Elisa.) Now, where were we?

Elisa: (Dumps her juice and screams again.)

Mother: (Looks at Elisa with irritation. Turns back to the phone.) Oh dear, she spilled her juice. Just a minute. (Puts down the phone and fixes another cup of juice. Sits with Elisa while she starts to drink it.)

Elisa: (Takes a swallow of juice.)

Mother: (Turns back to the phone.) Now, what were you saying?

Elisa: (Shoves the cup away from her and begins to cry and fuss again.)

Mother: (Extremely annoyed.) Just a minute. (Turns to Elisa.) What is it now, Elisa?

Elisa: (Tugs at her shoes.)

Mother: You want your shoes off. Okay, I'll help you. (Helps her take her shoes off.) Okay now, Elisa? Mommy wants to talk to Aunt Barbara now. (Turns back to the phone.)

Elisa: (Cries, whimpers, pulls at her mother, but gets no response. Tries harder—still no response.)

Mother: (Grits her teeth and yells into the phone.) Talk a little louder, will you? I can't hear you over all this racket.

Elisa: (Gives a final scream, then, sobbing, toddles off into the other room.)

Mother: (Sighs.) That's better. Now I can hear you. What were we talking about?

(Crash. A sound of breaking glass comes from the other room.)

Mother: (Looking extremely upset.) I have to go. Call you back later. (Hangs up and runs out.) Elisa, Elisa, are you okay? What happened, honey?

Poor mother was trying hard to juggle and she dropped the ball. In this scene the mother continually rewarded Elisa for behavior that seemed to bother her. She was effectively teaching Elisa to whine, fuss, spill juice, and break glass objects.

It's fairly easy to see that problems follow from rewarding undesirable behavior by paying attention to it. Surely the opposite is better—that is, rewarding desirable behavior. On the surface this approach seems to be a good one. When a child does something "good," something that pleases an adult, the adult is often full of praise. Sometimes people who live or work with young children are practically praise machines. Phrases like these are plentiful: "I'm so proud of you," "That's my girl," "Very good," "Wonderful," "Fantastic," "Good job." But what happens when the adult makes so much effort to control the child's behavior with praise? Some children may lose touch with their inner director, their own feelings and motives. They look around after every act to see if they did it right. They seek approval for everything they do. Activities are pleasing only for the rewards they bring him from the outside. In short, these children cease to get pleasure and satisfaction from the activities themselves.

Abraham Maslow, in his book *Toward a Psychology of Being*, states that when a child is faced with a conflict between inner delight at his own accomplishments and the rewards offered by others, he "must generally choose approval from others, and then handle his delight by repression or letting it die, or not noticing it or controlling it by willpower. In general, along with this will develop a disapproval of the delight experience, or shame and embarrassment and secretiveness about it, with finally, the inability even to experience it."[4]

Maslow is giving us a powerful message about the use of praise in infant education. His message is quite different from the common practice of many parents and caregivers, who lavish praise on children so they will feel good about themselves. Our experience is that children feel better about themselves when adults limit their praise and respond to successes with words like, "You must feel good about finally getting that shoe off," which are an attempt to acknowledge the child's own inner delight.

Feedback Part of infant education depends on the infant's getting clear feedback, that is, responses. Feedback comes both from the environment and from people. Children need to learn what effect their actions have on the world and on others. If they drop a glass of milk, it spills. If they cause their caregiver pleasure, pain, or anger, the caregiver feels good, or bad. Caregivers should express pleasure, pain, or anger in such a way that children understand the consequences of their actions. For example, the child who scratches the caregiver should be told clearly, "It hurts when you scratch me." If a child shows an act of kindness, such as picking up something the caregiver has dropped, the caregiver should state his feelings about the act. For instance, "Thank you for picking up my wallet, Ben. I appreciate it (or, it makes me feel good)."

Adults can also help provide feedback about the environment, as well as verbalizing the reaction they see in the child. In this way the child learns to give himself clear feedback. Here is an example of that principle.

Josh is playing with several other toddlers when his father arrives to pick him up at the center. As Josh rushes over, he slams his elbow into a table.

Josh: (Approaches his father crying.) Daddy, Daddy.
Father: Oh, Josh, I saw that. You bumped your elbow on the table.
Josh: (Holds his elbow up.) Me!
Father: Yes, right here. (Touches the spot gently.)
Josh: (Goes back to the table.) Table!

Father: Yes, right there. You bumped your elbow right there on the table. (Knocks on the table.)

Josh: (Touches the table.)

Father: The table is hard. It hurt when you hit your elbow on it.

Josh: Hard! (He cries less, concentrates on his elbow, then the table, then his elbow again.)

Josh's father helped him to focus on what just happened, and Josh learned something about cause and effect. Josh was shown what hurt him and gained some understanding of the relationship of the pain to the source. His father helped Josh to understand the full experience, rather than letting him get lost in the pain; yet he didn't deny his pain or distract him from it.

Think of a time in your own life when feedback was useful to you in a problem-solving situation. Write about it here.

Modeling   The last point we want to make here about the adult's role as infant educator is one that we have made before: *Practice, don't preach!* Model the behavior you want from the child. What you do speaks louder than what you say. For instance, if you want to teach the child to share, you need to *be* a sharing person yourself. You need to share your own possessions with others, if that's what you expect the baby to do. You can teach a baby to perform the actions of sharing with rewards and punishments, or you can *make* him share by using your size and power. But neither of these approaches will make the child a sharing person. He will become a sharing person (when given the freedom to decide whether or not to share) to the extent those around him (his models) are sharing people. In short, modeling behavior is more effective than "teaching" it.

Can you think of an example in your own life of modeling your behavior after someone else's? Did you consciously decide to act this way? Was the other person aware of your behavior? Did that person also teach you to act that way?

In summary, the adult role in infant education involves allowing for an appropriate degree of stress when a child is trying to solve a problem; responding appropriately to demands for attention; providing feedback; and modeling desirable behavior. The role of infant educator can be carried out at any time—during caregiving tasks or when babies are playing without direction.

Explaining infant education to people who think learning only comes from school-like activities is not easy. Consider how you would handle the following common situation.

A prospective parent comes to visit your center to look it over. She asks you, "Is this program educatonal? Do the babies learn anything or do they just play?"

What would you tell her?

The child's self-education   The word "education" comes from the latin word meaning to lead or draw out of, which suggests that there is something in the child that can be brought forth. That is quite a different concept from "putting something into the child." As we said at the beginning of this chapter, we believe that education is a process of facilitating the development and expression of the child's capabilities for problem solving. Let's look at an example of such capabilities. The child we are about to see is old enough to express the meaning of her actions in words, but the technique she is using has been developing since she was a toddler.

> *Robin:* (Agitated.) Mom, will you give me two dollars if I wash the car?
> *Mom:* No, it isn't worth that much to me.
> *Robin:* How about a dollar?
> *Mom:* I'm sorry, Robin, I just don't care a dollar's worth right now whether the car is clean or not.
> *Robin:* Well then, is it okay if I wash it for free?
> *Mom:* (Surprised.) Sure.
> *Robin:* (Mumbling as she goes out the door, rags in hand.) I just feel like messing around in water.

Robin has been "messing around in water" since infancy—waterplay in nursery school, playing in the sink and bath at home, and, as she got older, taking long baths, washing dishes, and watering plants. When life gets too hard to handle, something directs her toward the soothing qualities of water. She has found a valuable technique for solving the problem of calming herself when she is in emotional turmoil.

Look at an example of a child who has taught himself to get control over his feelings in another way. The feelings revealed here are not simple outward ones that come from frustrations, but are the often elusive unmanageable ones of dreams. Again this example is from an older child, who can say what goes on inside his head. They were reported by a nine-year-old, but the techniques were apparently worked out at a very young age.

Adam: I had a scary dream last night—full of monsters.
Mother: Oh?
Adam: Yes. It was awful, but I know I don't have to be afraid of dreams.
Mother: How's that?
Adam: Oh, I have a system. It's kind of complicated though . . . Do you want to hear about it?
Mother: Sure.
Adam: Well, whenever I have had a bad dream I just keep telling myself that I can always wake up.
Mother: That doesn't sound so complicated.
Adam: Oh, but that doesn't always work. So if the monsters keep on hanging around then I go on with this part.
Mother: What part?
Adam: Well, I have a picture of myself when I was in nursery school— remember the climbing thing in the play yard?
Mother: Yes.
Adam: Well, I have this picture of me way up on top of it. I'm with my friend, and down below us is a little kid on a tricycle.
Mother: Okay, but what does that have to do with the monsters in the dream?
Adam: I'm coming to that. See when the monsters get real bad then I bring a sort of TV set into my dream.
Mother: Uhuh.
Adam: Well, this is the easy part. I put the monsters on the TV set, see?
Mother: Yes . . .
Adam: Then a hand comes out, reaches over to the TV set and changes the channel.
Mother: What then?
Adam: That picture of me on the climbing thing comes on the screen, and then I don't have to be scared any more.
Mother: You've really got something there!

Without any sort of "how-to" instructions, this child has worked out for himself a way to get out of tough situations—at least in his dreams. He is able to control his own feelings with a rather sophisticated imagery device. Roberto Assagioli talks about this technique in his book, *The Act of Will*. He calls what Adam was doing the "technique of substitution."[5] Adam deliberately replaced the images causing him fear with an image of himself in a situation where he felt strong. With this image he in effect chased away the monsters.

Children can do much toward their own education process—even in infancy—without an adult facilitator. The capabilities even the youngest infant possesses are amazing. We will discuss this subject further in Chapter 9, when we talk about the development of a sense of self.

An example of infant education

The focus of this chapter has been on the adult role in facilitating infant education and to a lesser extent on the infant's own part. Kahlil Gibran has summed up the kind of relationship between the "educator" and the infant that we have presented: "If he is indeed wise he does not bid you enter the house of his wisdom, but rather leads you to the threshold of your own mind."[6]

To both illustrate and sum up our approach, we will take you into a center where the kind of infant education we have described is fostered. Notice how the principles we introduced in Chapter 1 are handled here in practice.

You're moving down a long hall in your mother's arms. You come to an open door, pass through it at shoulder height and find yourself in a familiar room. A quiet voice says your name and you look to the source. A short, white-haired woman with an energetic peacefulness about her looks you right in the eye and greets you.[7] You smile in return—you remember her from other visits.

You find yourself being carefully placed on a high, soft surface. Your mother's face appears above yours and she says something like, "I'm going to take your shoes off." You look around the room until your mother brings your attention to your foot, which has the shoe untied and loosened. You pull at it a little and it topples off. You laugh at this. You hear something about "the other one" and turn to discover the other foot is in the same condition. It's easy to pull this shoe off too.

You still have time to take things in while your mother talks to you and fiddles with your socks. Before you know it, you find a sock ready to be removed by you—and then another. Done. Nice accomplishment!

Before long you realize that you have helped to remove lots of restrictive things from your arms and legs. You feel air on your skin and lots of freedom. You're anxious to get off this high place and move. You wiggle around and find yourself carried down to the floor.

Now you're on a smooth, cool floor, sitting, staring at your mother's shins. Up you get on all fours, and without giving much thought to where you are going, you take off. You quickly notice a change under your knees. The smooth hard feeling has become soft and spongy. You stop for a moment to stick your fingers into the nap of a thick rug, then keep right on going past the designs on the rug, past a brightly colored scarf. You're headed for a shelf of toys you can see ahead of you.

Whoops, what is that? A face comes into view—a very small face and a pair of hands. You stop for a moment to investigate. You regard this face quietly and at the same time feel a big presence come up close beside you. You ignore this adult and reach for the face. You touch the smooth skin, and the eyes come to rest on you. You feel good. You pat the soft hair, then have an urge to know what the hair will feel like on your lips. You reach down and touch your lips to the hair.

You sense the pleasure of the adult sitting by you. You look up for a moment, but this big face isn't as appealing or as reachable as the small face on the floor by you. You move back to your examination of the face. Then you begin to get more energetic about your explorations and you feel a big hand stroking your small one, and you hear a voice saying "Gently, gently." You go back to your original soft stroking. Suddenly a small hand comes up and attaches itself to your hair. You move back, startled.

This movement puts you in a new position, and from this new place you can see a big, bright ball. You move over to it. You reach out and touch it—it rolls away from you. You feel excited about this and crawl after it. You try to hold it, but it keeps getting away from you.

You stop for a moment and take your bearings. You're far from the rug now, and the toy shelf you were originally after has disappeared completely. You find that the ball has rolled to a small bed with a doll inside. You reach for the doll, pick it up by one foot, and drop it. You take the blankets off the bed one by one, comparing their textures. When you get down to the hard bare wood, you figure you've seen enough and move on. As you pass by the doll you give a little attention to its face. You glance back to the small person on the rug, and a fleeting glimpse of that face crosses your mind. It's different from this one. You compare the two.

Suddenly you remember your mother. You have a tight feeling inside. Where is she? You sit straight up and look around. Not far away is a familiar pair of shoes and feet and legs. You look up and up until you get to her face. Her familiar voice says, "Yes, I'm still here." You crawl over and touch her skirt. Then you take off again.

You are aware now and then that there are other voices in the room. They talk softly and infrequently. You notice too that there are other people in the room. As you are about to go in pursuit of new adventures, you hear a squabble coming from a far corner of the room. You give your attention to it for a moment, but it makes no sense to you. You move on. You see an open door and you move toward it. On the way you pass a mirror and catch a glimpse of a familiar face. It's you! You pause momentarily to reacquaint yourself with your features.

Then the open door beckons again. As you go out you feel a change of texture under your hands and knees. You find yourself faced with the choice of a gently sloping ramp or low steps. You choose the ramp. You feel a downward pull as you crawl forward. At the end you feel warm grass under your hands and knees. It tickles a little. You sit quietly for a few minutes taking in the new sensations. Then you crawl a short distance and find yourself sitting in warm sand. You enjoy running your fingers through this new material for awhile.

Someone else is in the sandbox and you are about to poke a fat, soft leg, when you suddenly remember your mother again. Up the ramp and through the door you go, and you find her close by. Beside her is the toy shelf. You turn to move toward the shelf when your mother says, "I'm going into the other room now." You sit up wondering. You watch as your mother's feet get up and move slowly away. A feeling of distress comes over you, but you remain stunned. You want to do something to stop her, but you can't. Her feet disappear out the door and you can't see them any more.

You feel a tenseness in your face and a pounding in your ears. You hear a loud noise and feel something come out of your throat. You're all alone in the world. You have just enough time to fully react to this feeling when a hand touches you and says, "Your mother's right in the other room." You stop for a moment to consider what that means. But your mother doesn't come, so you get the same feeling back and your cries come pouring forth. The warm voice says, "You can go see your mother if you want." You don't really understand these words but the tone of voice captures your attention.

You stop crying, but then you start again because you're still stuck here without your mother, even though this other voice and hand are comforting. Then you see a big person, the one with the white hair, crawling in front of you, beckoning you to come. You begin to crawl and once you begin, you feel you can get to your mother! She isn't gone—she's reachable! You move with energy out the door into the other room. There are those wonderful familiar feet! You crawl over to them, hugging the shins. Your mother comes down to you. She touches you and says, "Here I am. You were upset because you couldn't find me."

You sit down on the floor and bask in her presence. But very shortly you get the urge to go back into the room with the toys and the white-haired woman. You move awa from your mother and start back. You watch her from time to time, but she doesn't move. You move out of sight of her but have the feeling that you can get to her again.

As you pass back through the door you see a big, soft, floppy ball. It's a beach ball only half blown up. You reach out for it and grab it in your hand.

Just as you are about to enjoy it, you find it in the hands of someone else. You are surprised and disappointed at the same time. You reach for it—but the person moves away. You follow and reach again. You just get your fingertips on it when it suddenly is yanked away again. You sit back in tears. It feels as if you are going to cry for a very long time. You have just settled back to do that when a hand touches you and a voice says, "You don't like it when Kevin takes the ball." Such understanding is conveyed by that voice that your feeling about having a long cry changes. Now that you have shared your feeling you don't have to hang onto it. You cry a few more sobs, look at the face, and let go of the feeling.

You move away toward a low table. As you come up to the table you see the underside first. The paint is missing here and there and the textures are interesting. You wonder what is on top. You pull yourself up to have a look. There is a puzzle. Another child, Kevin, is just removing two pieces. You push the puzzle with your hand and it falls on the floor with a great big delightful noise. Kevin looks at the puzzle, then at you. You take the piece he has in his hand. He looks surprised. You pick up a piece on the floor and begin to bang the two together. You feel that Kevin wants to take the piece back, but he makes no move to do so. He leaves you in peace and you shove the puzzle under the table and then follow it. You turn on your back and contemplate the textures of the unpainted side of the table. A feeling of real peace comes over you and you spend a long time there.

When you're ready, you crawl out and look around. You spy Kevin again. He is climbing on a low platform. You find that interesting and start over in his direction. By the time you get there the platform is empty. You want very much to get up on it, but you don't know how. You make several attempts to crawl up, but it is just a little bit too high. You are just about to give up when a voice says, "Maybe a cushion will make it easier for you." A flat, firm cushion appears between you and the platform. You sit back to think this over—but only for a minute. You climb up on the cushion and from there you can easily get onto the platform.

What a great feeling to be up there! You take only a moment to let it sink in and then crawl back down. You want to try to get up there again. You manage the climb again and get the same feeling. You repeat this sequence a number of times until the pleasure of it begins to wear off.

You are just beginning to wonder whether you should stop or not when you become aware of some fussing noises in another part of the room. You stop to take in what is happening there. An adult is talking to a fussy baby. You hear the word "juice," which reminds you of a little feeling that you've been having down inside. You look over to where you remember the snack cupboard is. Sure enough, there is the white-haired woman helping Kevin wheel the snack cupboard over to the table you were lying under earlier.

You get very excited and start for the table. But you forget you were on the little platform. You miss the cushion and find yourself sprawled on the floor. You're surprised and upset. You let out a loud series of cries. You have your eyes closed, so you don't see an adult come to your side. Instead, you feel a calming presence. You open your eyes and hear a voice say, "You fell down." You lie there a moment, gathering together your scattered feelings before you attempt to pick yourself up. The adult waits. You wait. The adult says, "Do you need some help?" You take a quick inventory, move an arm, shake your leg, and discover that all your parts still work. You pull yourself together, rejecting the offer of help.

An image of your mother flashes across your mind and you think you might need her very much right in the next instant. But the table and juice come to your mind, and you remember what is to come. You continue on your way, vaguely aware of a little sensation in your leg that wasn't there before, as well as a slight throbbing in one cheek. As you get to the table you feel (or perhaps hear) a welcome. You get into a chair by yourself and sit back to see what will happen next.

This infant encountered some problems that could be solved alone and some that required help. The adults were both active and receptive. The infant felt some stress, but never so much that it prevented problem solving. Needs for attention (which were never very great in this scene) were satisfied in ways that did nothing to encourage undesirable behavior. The infant received feedback—both from actions on the objects in the environment and from the adults present. And the adults consistently modeled the behavior they wanted to "teach."

Could you do as well as the adults in this center? Rate yourself as a caregiver. Start by making a list of skills or competencies you think a caregiver in the center described above should have. Write that list here.

Now compare your list with ours. Rate yourself on each item by checking yes, no, or not sure. Add other appropriate skills.

	Yes	No	Not Sure
I can pay full attention to an infant, when appropriate to do so, during a problem-solving situation.	____	____	_____
I can be both responsive and directive when it is appropriate.	____	____	_____
I can distinguish optimum stress from too much stress and can make appropriate decisions about when to intervene.	____	____	_____
I can satisfy a baby's need for attention in ways that encourage development and socially acceptable behavior.	____	____	_____
I can give feedback when it is appropriate.	____	____	_____
I can model the behavior I wish to see in the baby.	____	____	_____

I can . . .

I can . . .

I can . . .

Notes

1 T. Berry Brazelton, M.D., with Mary Main, "Are There Too Many Sights and Sounds in Your Baby's World?" *Redbook,* September 1971.

2 The idea for this exercise and the preceding one was suggested by Jack Canfield and Harold Wells in *100 Ways to Enhance Self-Concept in the Classroom* (Englewood Cliffs: Prentice-Hall, 1976).

3 Personal letter from Patti Wade, October 1978.

4 Abraham H. Maslow, *Toward a Psychology of Being,* 2d ed. (New York: D. van Nostrand Company, 1968), p.51. © 1968 by Litton Educational Publishing, Inc. Reprinted by permission of D. van Nostrand Company.

5 Roberto Assagioli, *The Act of Will* (Baltimore: Penguin Books, 1973).

6 Kahlil Gibran, *The Prophet* (New York: Alfred A. Knopf, 1965), p. 56.

7 Magda Gerber, The infant center you are touring is the Demonstration Infant Program.

Further reading

Fraiberg, Selma H. *The Magic Years.* New York: Charles Scribner's Sons, 1959.

Fromm, Erich. *The Art of Loving.* New York: Bantam Books, 1956.

Ginott, Haim G. *Between Parent and Child.* New York: Macmillan, 1965.

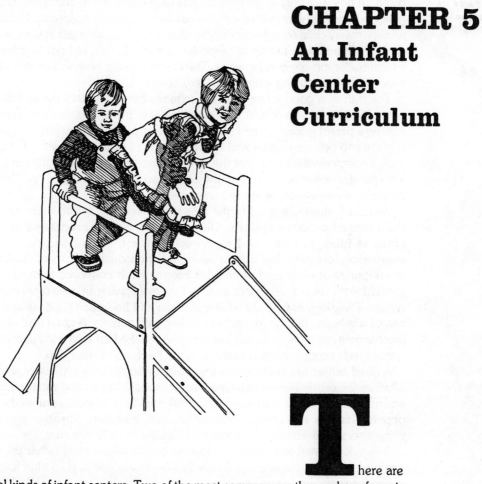

CHAPTER 5
An Infant Center Curriculum

There are several kinds of infant centers. Two of the most common are those whose focus is day care (for infants whose parents cannot care for them at home during the day) and those whose focus is education (infant education and/or parent education). The educational programs may be for normal infants, at-risk infants (i.e., infants who may not develop normally), or infants with identified developmental disabilities. The two kinds of programs may overlap. That is, day care programs usually have a parent education component and education programs may also include day care. This chapter describes a day care program, but the principles of curriculum design outlined here will fit any type of infant program.

The characteristics of a good infant center
What are the characteristics of a good infant center? The long scene at the end of Chapter 4 showed some of them. Most notable perhaps was the pace. Things happened slowly—the pace was an infant one, not an adult one. The child had

65

plenty of time not only to grasp what was happening but to anticipate what was going to happen. Along with the slow pace went a quiet atmosphere. The sounds were primarily child sounds rather than adult ones. The adult talk in the scene was quality talk and was mostly in response to a child. Talk did not interfere with concentration on direct experience. The children could be involved in their own concerns without being interrupted very often.

The staff of a good infant center recognizes how important the parent-infant relationship is. It looks at itself as a supplement to the family, not a replacement. Having a parent education and involvement component of any program ensures that the gap between center and home remains as small as possible. The aim of such a component is to see that the values, cultures, and goals of the parents are incorporated into the running of the center, so that the children see life at the center as an extension of life at home.

Another feature of a good center is its record keeping, which is also related to the parent education component. Observations of how an infant is growing in his ability to relate to others and to the environment, as well as developmental information, can be a big help in seeing the individual patterns of growth and development of each child. When this information is conveyed to parents, they can add to the record with information of their own, giving an even more complete picture. Daily logs of who ate what and when and how each child felt and acted can be a valuable vehicle for communicating with parents. A good deal of parent involvement happens as the child arrives and is picked up. That kind of consistent contact with caregivers does much to close the home-center gap.

A good center has goals. Goals that have to do with the type of care include whether the center has an individualized approach, health and safety, nutrition, and nurturance. Goals that have to do with the kind of experiences offered include opportunities for free choice, exploration, both individual attention and group experiences, and above all, variety and balance in daily activities.

A developmental approach that focuses on the whole child rather than on a single aspect of development (e.g., intellectual development) is another feature of a good center. Age-appropriate activities and equipment let each child feel comfortable, yet be challenged. The appendix of this book consists of a chart laying out six developmental levels as well as the kinds of equipment, toys, and adult approaches that go with each.

Lastly, the smooth running of a good center depends on its staff relations. Provision should be made for the staff to receive on-going training and support. Through supportive supervision and regular meetings, a supervisor who is skilled at promoting good human relations can cultivate rapport among the staff. These and other good relationships among adults are models for the children.

Interaction as curriculum

The most important characteristic of a good center is its curriculum, its plan for learning. A good infant center views its curriculum primarily as interactions. Interactions can be divided into two categories: (1) interaction between the infant and the other people in the center, and (2) interaction between the infant and the environment. We will first look at interactions with people. Then we will consider the importance of a prepared environment.

Personal interaction Interaction between infants and caregivers is, as we said above, a vital part of the curriculum. A good center provides for the infants' attachment needs by assigning one caregiver to several infants. The idea behind this is that if a caregiver sees three or four children as his or her special charges, he or she can promote a stronger attachment than might happen if attachment were left to chance. Naturally shifts change and caregivers come and go. Nevertheless, if attachment needs are recognized, much can be done to provide for them.

In the following scene with eight infants and two caregivers, consistent feeding by one caregiver, who is released from other duties to give her full attention to the baby she is feeding, promotes attachment. Notice in this scene not only how the caregiver builds attachment, but also how the children use their attachment to the *other* caregiver. When a threatening situation arises (for instance, when a stranger walks into the room) the children head for the person to whom they are attached.

A slender middle-aged woman is sitting low in a bean bag chair. On her lap is a baby who has climbed there to pat her cheek. Clinging to her shoulder is a toddler who is also trying to climb on her lap. The baby pushes gently at the toddler to try to keep him off. "No," says the toddler, who continues to hang on tight. A short distance away two toddlers are banging wooden spoons on empty margarine cartons. A third child sits looking on, quietly opening and closing a small cardboard box that has a big plastic bead inside. Just beyond the seated woman is a large pen that fences off one corner of the room. In it two very young infants are lying on their backs, waving their arms and looking at each other and at the scattering of toys close to them. In another area of the room a man is seated in a comfortable chair, quietly giving a baby his bottle. His full attention is on the baby he is feeding, while the woman is obviously taking charge of all the rest of the children in the room. She focuses on the two children interacting with her, but she also manages to spread her attention to the other children.

A man walks into the room. All action immediately stops except the arm waving in the one corner and the feeding in the other. The climbers and the bangers sit with their eyes on the stranger. The child who had been watching the bangers starts creeping backwards toward the woman in the bean bag chair, never taking her eyes off the man's face. When she reaches the comfort and safety of the familiar lap, she climbs on, clutching at her caregiver's blouse. The woman puts her arm reassuringly around the child and speaks first to her and then to the man. "That's Josh's father, Melanie," she says matter-of-factly. Then to the man, "Hello David. You're early today. Josh is still in the nap room, but he is probably just about starting to wake up. Oh, by the way, be sure to check his log—he didn't eat much lunch today—see what's written down. He may be really ready for something to eat when he gets home. Also, as I recall, he was tired this morning, but couldn't sleep. He's been grumpy all day, but had a long nap this afternoon.''

The man thanks her and leaves the room to get his son. The action starts up again. Melanie crawls down and goes back to her cardboard box. In the corner pen both infants have started whimpering, and one occasionally breaks into a loud cry. The woman gets up, telling the children around her that she is going to do so beforehand. She goes into the pen to talk to the two needy babies. "Yes, I know Nathan," she says to the one crying loudest, "you need to eat. I'm going to feed you just as soon as Daryl finishes and can take over for me." And then turning to the other child, who has settled down a bit with her presence—"And then it's your turn to eat. I don't think you're too hungry yet, are you?" Turning back to the first infant, "It's hard to wait, I know.''

Notice that this scene showed examples of most of the goals we mentioned above. Notice, too, that in this center caregivers kept daily logs on "their" children so that at least one person could give a comprehensive and detailed report to parents when they arrived to pick them up. This record keeping also served to make the caregivers pay special attention to "their" children.

Infants learn from their peers as well as from adults. By interacting with their peers, infants learn much about the world, their power in it, and their effect on others. As they explore their environment and each other, they eventually come to find out the difference between themselves and other people as well as the difference between objects and people. Through the kinds of problem-solving situations that present themselves in infant-infant interactions, children come to learn such valuable skills as how to resolve conflicts. By selective intervention, caregivers help bring this learning about. Selective intervention means that caregivers help children out only when they are likely to hurt themselves or others or when they are obviously not able to work toward their own solution.

The prepared environment A good center understands the importance of a prepared environment. Ideally the indoor setting allows for activity areas that are distinct from each other: areas for diapering, feeding, playing, sleeping, staff, visiting parents, and the office. The children are divided into reasonable-size groups (12 is our own preference) and are in rooms that are of a size appropriate to the group—not crowded but not too large. (California state law requires 35 square feet of indoor space for each infant.) There should be open areas in the room, and traffic patterns should not interfere with activities. Safety, of course, is a primary consideration in setting up the environment. If the children in the center are of mixed ages, there should be different areas for children of each developmental stage: those who are still immobile, those who move by rolling, those who can creep and crawl, those who cruise, those who walk, and those who can run and ride wheeled toys.

The outdoor environment is as important as the indoor environment. If possible, children should be able to come and go as they please. A variety of surfaces should be available—some grass and other soft surfaces, some smooth hard surfaces, and a hard area for wheeled toys. It is nice when a yard can have some growing things in it, as well as both shade and sun. As indoors, a variety of levels is desirable—for example, hills, platforms, decks, and climbing equipment.

When we discuss play as curriculum, we will give an example of an environment that is divided into areas for children of different stages of development and describe the variety that this environment offers.

We have looked at the curriculum as two sets of interactions: interactions between infants and other people, and interactions between the infants and the environment. Now let us look at curriculum from a different point of view. Another way to regard curriculum is to look at the kinds of activities it comprises—for instance, caregiving (feeding, diapering and so forth) and play. Nearly everything that happens in a center fits into one of these two categories.

Caregiving as curriculum

We have emphasized the importance of the adult's attitude toward caregiving in previous chapters. It is during times when the infant has full adult attention on himself alone that much learning takes place. Diapering, for example, is not a chore but a vital part of the curriculum. Lifelong learnings and attitudes can be initiated on the diapering table. Likewise, feeding is another vital part of the curriculum. Not only does it promote attachment between infant and caregiver, it provides a variety of sensory experiences, much pleasure and satisfaction, and an opportunity to learn social and eventually self-help skills. Dressing, grooming, and washing are other opportunities for promoting attachment, providing sensory experiences, and developing self-help skills.

Consider the following situation. What would you do to get this child diapered?

You are a caregiver in an infant center. You are trying to diaper Maria who is ten months old and a headache to diaper because she twists and squirms and wiggles so much. Right now she is trying to crawl off the diapering table.

How would you make diapering this child an educational experience, a part of the curriculum?

Play as curriculum

The main ingredient of any infant program, whether day care or educational center, should be play. Play has long been recognized by early childhood educators as vital to growth and learning. It is natural to babies and should be regarded as an *important* use of their time, not as something secondary or optional.

Play offers the baby opportunities that come from nowhere else. Through play babies get involved in open-ended exploration. They are not confined by rules, procedures, or outcomes. Children at play have self direction—it might be said that they have power. Through total absorption during play they make discoveries they might otherwise never make; they work on problems, they make choices, and they find out what interests them. The scene at the end of Chapter 4 showed many examples of how babies play.

The role of the adult in infant play goes from "hands off" to active involvement. The adult may be part of the play, but if he is, he cannot play for particular results, or the play ceases to be play. If the adult is not a part of the play, a policy of minimal interference ensures that the child remains in control as well as totally absorbed. Examples of how the adult acts in these two roles were also shown in the infant center scene at the end of Chapter 4.

Any infant center curriculum should provide for, and indeed promote, a good deal of play. Unfortunately, not all parents or infant caregivers are aware of its importance. We have visited a number of programs structured in such a way that the children were so involved in adult-directed "learning activities" that they could only play when they could escape the adults' notice. The adults saw their role as *teaching* rather than *facilitating* infant learning, and therefore they remained in control of what happened most of the time.

The way to promote play is to provide the time and space for it without a lot of adult interference, and very little adult direction. The adult's role is to set up the environment so that it is conducive to play. Environment here means both the physical setting (including defined space, toys, and furniture) and the emotional setting (which includes caregivers' attitudes). The social setting is also part of the environment; it includes the size of the groups and the age mixture of the children.

The environment should be set up to provide choices. Free choice is an important ingredient of play. (It is also an important prerequisite to learning.) J. McVicker Hunt talks about the relationship of learning to choice in terms of what he calls the "problem of the match." He says that learning occurs when the environment provides experiences just familiar enough that the child can understand them with the mental ability he has already attained but just new enough to offer interesting challenges.[1]

Learning occurs when there is optimum incongruity between what is already known and a new situation. If the situation is too new and different, the child withdraws, becomes frightened, ignores it, or reacts in some way other than learning. If it is not novel enough, the child ignores it. He won't pay attention to that which has already become so much a part of him that it no longer "registers."

Look at an example showing these principles.

Angela is lying on a rug in the infant room of her day care center. A caregiver is nearby. On the wall, low down, obviously put there for her to look at, is a picture of a face. From the look of the picture and its curled edges, it has been in that same spot for some time. Angela pays no attention to it, even though when it was first hung up she found it interesting. She is playing with a bit of fuzz that has come off the blanket she is lying on, ignoring the bright-colored scarf on the floor near her. The door of the room opens and a preschool-age boy bounds in announcing to the caregiver, "My teacher said I could come and show my sister my Halloween costume." Angela looks up at the noise just in time to see her brother put a bear mask on his face. She had been ready to smile, but now her eyes reflect sheer terror. Her mouth opens wide, and as soon as she can manage it a huge scream issues forth, which startles the other infants in the room. The boy takes off the mask immediately and hides it behind his back. The caregiver tries to calm Angela by showing her that it is just a mask, but she won't allow the thing to come near her. Finally the mask is put away and Angela quiets down. Peace is restored as the other infants settle back, unaware of the details of what has happened. A few minutes later a little girl comes in looking for the boy, who is playing with Angela now. She has two red spots painted on her cheeks, big freckles on her nose, and lipstick on her mouth. She goes over to Angela and bends down. Angela is intrigued with the change in the familiar face, and as the scene closes she is poking her finger at the red spots and smearing the freckles.

The question is, how can we set up an environment so that it has elements of "optimum incongruence?" How do we know exactly what a match is for an infant? How can we match the problems with the immediate stage of development of the child? All we can do is provide a number of choices of appropriate toys, objects, and activities and let the child play. Given the chance, children will naturally move to novel situations and novel uses of materials. They have a need to learn, a desire to understand. We can therefore let their needs and desires guide their use of the environment. By directing them with either praise or punishment (or pressure of any sort) we distract them from the inner delights mentioned by Maslow in Chapter 4. Children get these inner delights from struggling with a problem that matches their learning level.

Sooner or later a child with an interesting, challenging environment is bound to find a problem that he wants to solve, but can't. Magda Gerber calls this situation "getting stuck." A child is stuck when he cannot figure out the next move. The adult can then step in and provide the smallest possible bit of help—the tiny link that allows the child to move forward again. This help is the selective intervention mentioned earlier. It's hard to know exactly when to step in. If the adult steps in too soon, the child gets little satisfaction. If the adult steps in too late, the child may have already given up. It's also hard to know just how much help to provide. We have observed that most of the time most of us are tempted to step in too soon with too much help. We should resist this tendency if we are to provide the best learning opportunities for the child.

Take a look at "getting stuck" from another point of view. Sometimes a child gets stuck by becoming satiated with something. He has had enough of some activity or some level of development. *We* decide that he is bored and we want to do something about it—quickly! Many adults have a great fear of boredom for infants as well as for themselves. This fear has perhaps been heightened by the recent vogue for infant stimulation. Yet boredom is educational and can be considered part of the learning plan of any program. See what Maslow says:

> The single holistic principle that binds together the multiplicity of human motives is the tendency for a new and higher need to emerge as the lower need fulfills itself by being sufficiently gratified. The child who is fortunate enough to grow normally and well gets satiated and *bored* with the delights that he has savored sufficiently, and *eagerly* (without pushing) goes on to higher, more complex, delights as they become available to him without danger or threat . . .
> . . . He doesn't have to be "kicked upstairs," or forced on to maturity as is so often implied. He *chooses* to grow on to higher delights, to become bored with older ones. [2]

Children cannot push on until they have done very thoroughly what it is that they need to do. Until they have reached the state of boredom, they are still motivated by unfinished business. They can't move on. Boredom, when they finally attain it, provides the push to move on—but the push comes from within, not from without. They can then leave behind the old level, the old needs, and deal with the new ones, giving them their full attention. When the push to move on comes from without—from the adult or the environment—children never quite satisfy themselves. They may move on to the next stage, task, or activity with leftover feelings from the previous one, perhaps unable to give full attention to the new.

This idea of children deciding for themselves when to move on is the basis of the play yard designs of Jerry Ferguson, who is an architect as well as an early childhood educator. [3] Ferguson designs environments uniquely suited to allowing infants to decide when and whether they are old enough to leave each developmental area. For example, she designed a play yard for the Pacific Oaks Infant-Toddler Program in Pasadena, California. In that play yard the very youngest infants were in a low stimulation area in the middle yard but cut off from the rest by a variety of barriers. In this area was a grassy place, completely safe for tiny babies. Beyond the grass was a sandy place with a tunnel at the end connecting the sand to a still more challenging play yard. Between the grass and the sand there was also a low wooden walkway designed to present a sufficient barrier to infants who were not yet ready to cross it. Children who were just beginning to move around had to conquer the raised walkway before they would get to the sand. They could test the sand from the safety of the walk before deciding to go into it, and they did this, sometimes for a week at a time, before they were ready. By the time they chose to go into the sand, they were able to handle the risks it presented, and the sand then became a safe environment for them. The tunnel at the other end, though obviously open, presented a formidable barricade, and few children chose to go through it until they were nearly ready to walk.

Thus, by the time the infants were able to leave the safe inner yard (by their own choice), they were developmentally ready for the bigger challenges of the yard beyond. This yard was designed for the beginning walker and good crawler and was interesting and safe, yet challenging (i.e., optimally risky). Beyond was the most challenging yard, with climbing equipment and wheeled toys for the older children. Although all the children who left the inner yard could return to it, few did so except for occasional visits. They chose to play where the environment had more to offer them.

Jerry Ferguson stresses that her approach works only because the infants have learned to take some responsibility for their own well-being. They come to depend on their ability to make choices, which means they have had the opportunity to gain experience in making decisions.

In this chapter we have laid out the characteristics of a good infant center: a quiet, peaceful atmosphere; parent education and involvement; record keeping; goals; a developmental approach; and good staff relations. We have also examined the definitions and elements of a curriculum for an infant center. We have defined curriculum as interactions (with people and objects), caregiving, and play.

Now we would like to ask you to rate your abilities to set up an infant center curriculum yourself. Can you finish the following sentences?

I can provide a safe and healthy learning environment by:

I can promote physical and intellectual competency by:

I can promote language development by:

I can build a positive self-image by:

I can help the infant become a social being by:

When you have finished, you can see how your suggestions compare with ours by turning to the appendix, which compiles ideas for promoting physical, intellectual, language, and social-emotional development at six stages of growth.

Notes

1 J. McVicker Hunt, *Intelligence and Experience* (New York: The Ronald Press, 1961), p. 267.

2 Jerry Ferguson, "Creating Growth-Producing Environments for Infants and Toddlers," in E. Jones, ed., *Supporting the Growth of Infants, Toddlers, and Parents* (Pasadena, Ca.: Pacific Oaks College, 1979).

3 Abraham H. Maslow, *Toward a Psychology of Being,* 2d ed. (New York: D. van Nostrand Company, 1968), pp. 55-56. © 1968 by Litton Educational Publishing, Inc.

Further reading

Dittman, L. *The Infants We Care For.* Washington, D.C.: National Association for the Education of Young Children, 1973.

Jones, Elizabeth. *Dimensions of Teaching-Learning Environments.* Pasadena: Pacific Oaks College, 1973.

Jones, Elizabeth, ed. *Supporting the Growth of Infants, Toddlers, and Parents.* Pasadena: Pacific Oaks College, 1979.

Provence, S., et al. "The Day-to-Day Experience for Infants and Toddlers," in *The Challenge of Day Care.* New Haven: Yale University Press, 1977.

PART II

Focus on the Infant

CHAPTER 6
The Development of Attachment

Once the umbilical cord has been cut, the newborn is a separate individual. His life depends on the attention, the care, and the love of those around him. The ability an infant has to bring persons close to him—for example, through crying, clinging, and grasping—in order to receive this care and attention is the beginning of the process called attachment. It is important to emphasize that attachment is an ongoing process that brings individuals together and allows them to stay together. To be attached to someone assumes trust in the bond or relationship between oneself and another.

Attachment between infant and caregiver can be seen as a continuum involving attention-getting, fear and anxiety, dependency, exploration, and autonomous behavior. No one behavior in this process can be seen as completely separate from the next, nor can any one behavior be used exclusively as the definition of "attachment." Attachment begins in the infant in the form of "proximity-seeking behavior," but it rapidly expands and eventually allows the person to be self-reliant and independent. To appreciate this complex process it is important to look at it in more detail.

How attachment develops

Think for a moment about the cry of the newborn. That cry almost invariably elicits an emotion in the people who hear it. It is hard to ignore. At once it becomes one of the strongest signals an infant makes to the people responsible for its care.

Other behaviors, too, bring forth emotional responses. Some of them are revealed in the following scene:

A young mother is working in the kitchen. There is a steady and insistent crying in the background. Several pots are bubbling on the stove. The mother checks under the lids, turns down the heat to simmer, and, as the cries become louder, gives a last glance to see that things can wait for her attention awhile. We follow her into the other room where she hastens to a bassinet. Her attention is completely directed toward the small person inside. She talks soothingly as she bends over with her arms outstretched.

Mother: I know you are hungry. Here I am. I'm sorry you had to wait.
Baby: (Ceases crying at the sound of the voice. Then cries even harder.)
Mother: I know. Yes, yes, I know. I'm going to pick you up now so you can eat.
Baby: (Continues to scream.)
Mother: (Picks him up. Settles in a comfortable chair and prepares to nurse.)
Baby: (Stops screaming. Begins to squirm and root frantically as soon as he feels his mother's warmth and closeness.)
Mother: There you are. That's better isn't it.
Baby: (Eyes tightly closed, fists clenched, sucks furiously.)
Mother: (Settles back and moves around until she is comfortable.)
Baby: (Begins to relax a bit, but does not ease up on the sucking.)
Mother: You were really hungry, weren't you?
Baby: (Continues to suck without stopping.)
Mother: (Sits back looking relaxed and contented.)
Baby: (Eases up a little. His fists unclench, and one hand reaches out, groping.)
Mother: (Touches his hand with her finger.)
Baby: (Wraps his fingers around her finger and holds on tight.)
Mother: (Snuggles him a little closer and kisses the top of his head.)
Baby: (Opens his eyes and looks up at her.)
Mother: (Looks back with warmth and love.)
Baby: (Stops sucking momentarily. With his gaze fixed on his mother's eyes, his mouth breaks into a big smile.)
Mother: (Smiles back.)
Baby: (Snuggllgles in even closer and continues to suck contentedly, his little fist wrapped around her finger, his eyes looking into hers.)

These two are a unit. Both feel that this is an intimate moment of a close partnership. The infant has the capacity to elicit delight from another; this in turn gives him pleasure. The example of the feeding experience illustrates some of the repertoire of behaviors involved in attachment. Through these mutually responsive behaviors, which included touching, fondling, and eye contact, as well as feeding, the infant and the adult form an extremely close relationship. The infant needs this relationship because he cannot physically attach himself to any person or persons who will nourish and care for him.

Very early the baby begins to react differently to the person(s) of his attachment than to other people. He starts by sorting out the difference between people and objects and goes on to distinguish between his special person(s) and other people. Within the first few months of life the baby can clearly indicate recognition of his mother (or other primary caregiver). At first he follows her with his gaze, sometimes crying when she leaves, and later, when he is mobile, he crawls after her in preference to others. This ability to show reliance on others and trust in their willingness to meet his needs is the beginning of dependency, and dependency is another important aspect of attachment.

Once infants begin to realize what they need and who the persons are who can satisfy their needs, they develop additional behaviors. Some of these behaviors express frustration and may be hard for adults to handle; therefore it can be helpful for the caregivers to know what is happening in the infant's development.

How attachment grows and changes

Important milestones of mental and social development are reached when infants begin to discriminate between just any human face and familiar faces. Babies who grow up in nonnurturing environments do not reach these milestones. They respond indiscriminately. If they feel no attachment, they apparently feel no need to distinguish one person from another (although whether they cannot or are not interested, we do not know).

Once babies can distinguish their mother or caregiver from other people, two new worries begin. One, at about eight to ten months of age they begin to fear strangers. Two, now that they know who mother is, they worry about losing her. This latter fear usually appears by about ten to twelve months. Both of these fears indicate infants' ability to discriminate and recognize difference and are therefore obvious signs of mental growth. Corresponding to this second developmental fear is their inability to understand that objects that are gone from sight still exist. Piaget called this concept "object permanancy"; it will be discussed further in Chapter 9. The infant's worry about losing his mother is understandable. He cannot foresee that a separation is only temporary. Knowing this, it is easier for caregivers to understand the desperation of the protest when a baby is left behind as mother walks out the door.

It may be helpful here to emphasize the interplay between dependency, mental development, and trust in this process of attachment. When an eighteen-month-old child is clinging to his mother and crying for her not to go (obvious dependent behavior), he is also saying I *know* I need you (a mental function). As his mental capacity grows and his experiences teach him that he can trust his mother to return, it will be easier and easier for him to let go and become more autonomous. This ability to trust a relationship is the foundation for independence.

Another implication of attachment for mental development has to do with exploratory behavior. Babies who know they have a bond with their caregiver seem to feel freer to move out into new territory. They can move away from the caregiver with greater ease than babies who cannot trust the relationship. As children move out into the environment, they find novelty, problems, and stimulation, which encourages them to move out even more. They make discoveries; they learn.

Twenty years ago the psychologist Harry Harlow showed how the relationship between attachment and exploratory behavior worked with baby monkeys. He used surrogate mothers made of wire and terry cloth to which the babies became attached in the absence of the real mother. If one of these baby monkeys was placed in a strange room alone, it would cower fearfully in a corner, not moving around. When the terry cloth ''mother'' was put in the room with him, the baby would run to it and cling until he was brave enough to venture out and explore the room. He would return now and then to cling and reassure himself that his ''mother'' was still there, as if to recharge himself with courage. The difference in exploratory behavior with and without the object of attachment present was obvious.

Take a look at how some of the concepts discussed appear in human infants:

Several mothers and their babies are sitting on a floor among a scattering of toys, low furniture, bean bag chairs, and rugs. The room is fairly quiet except for occasional baby noises. Then a hammering sound can be heard, and a girl about 10 months old clutches her mother's knees while looking intently at a 14-month-old girl who is using a hammer on a toy pounding bench.

Mother: (Speaking to the child clinging to her.) Do you want to see what Kim is doing?

Susan: (Looks at her mother and tries to climb her like a vine.)

Mother: (Puts her arm around Susan.)

Susan: (Looks at Kim, makes a murmuring noise, and continues to cling.)

Mother: (Takes her hand away, pats Susan on the back, and leans back, leaving Susan free to let go and move away.)

Susan: (Loosens her grip on her mother.)

Mother: (Remains quiet and lets her go.)

Susan: (Starts off across the floor cautiously toward Kim and the pounding noise. She freezes as another adult enters the room. She backs toward her mother keeping her eye on the new adult. The adult turns and moves toward Kim and away from Susan. Susan pauses. The adult moves on across the room, and Susan continues her journey toward Kim.)

Kim: (Notices Susan. Stops pounding.)

Susan: (Proceeds with even more caution than before.)

Kim: (Notices a beach ball a few feet away, gets up, and moves quickly toward it.)

Susan: (Watches Kim move away from the pounding bench. She moves to the abandoned toy and examines it carefully, first with her eyes, then with her hands, and finally pushes and shoves it, making a noise of wood against vinyl.)

Kim: (Hears the noise and starts back toward the toy she had abandoned.)

Susan: (Freezes.)

Kim: (Reaches Susan quickly and holds out a hand as though she might take the toy from her.)

Susan: (Drops the toy and flees back to the safety of her mother. This time instead of clinging to her, she stays by her, laying one hand on her leg, remaining close, but barely touching.)

Kim: (Moves away from the toy again.)

Susan: (Starts for the toy, more quickly this time.)

The scene freezes on Susan pounding contentedly on the toy bench, which she has moved over near her mother.

So far, we have seen Susan gradually become more independent in her explorations as the result of being able to "touch home base" when she needs to. Her mother is available for support and strength and provides the security she needs to venture away from her. Susan is building trust. Let's pick up the scene where we left off.

Susan is pounding on the bench near her mother.

Mother: I'm going into the other room now, Susan.

Susan: (Gives no indication that she has heard.)

Mother: (Starts toward the door, then stops, realizing that Susan is preoccupied and has not heard her or noticed that she is leaving.) Susan . . .

Susan: (Stops pounding and looks at her mother.)

Mother: I'm going into the other room now. I'll be back soon.

Susan: (Remains suspended.)

Mother: (Leaves without hesitation.)

Susan: (Remains frozen for a short period. Then her face begins to cloud up. She starts after her mother, stops, looks around, and can no longer see her. A howl of protest comes forth.)

The adult who walked into the room earlier moves toward Susan slowly.

Adult: Your mother is in the other room, Susan.

Susan: (Looks at her with deep suspicion and howls louder in the direction her mother has gone.)

Mother: (Reappearing briefly in the doorway.) Susan, I'm here.
Susan: (Moves forward like a shot, out the door to her mother.)

Notice how trust was built, and how Susan was given a chance to work both on her fear of being separated from her mother and on solving her own problems. Although she was being separated from her mother, she was able to discover where her mother was and to get to her on her own. Notice too that Susan had warning that her mother was leaving. Her mother did not sneak away while Susan was distracted. Susan learns from this approach that her mother does not come and go without warning, but rather that her departure is predictable, at least to the extent that it follows a "good-bye" ritual. Thus, Susan learns to confine her worries to the times of actual separation rather than wondering constantly and uneasily whether or not her mother has slipped out on her.

Susan has just mastered one more step toward understanding that the relationship with her mother is to be trusted. It stretches, but it holds. Furthermore she is coming to see herself as a capable problem solver, an attitude that will, in turn, greatly affect the development of her problem-solving skills later, whether they be for handling social, physical, emotional, or intellectual problems.

It is important that infants trust the relationships in their environment and it is important that they be helped to meet their own needs when they can (e.g., Susan finding her mother). For trusting relationships to develop, caregivers must be responsive—must be sensitive to what the baby is communicating about his needs as well as to his obvious needs. Nevertheless, it is important not to be *overresponsive*. Overresponding prevents the baby from seeing himself as a capable person able to soothe himself, solve some of his own problems, and learn to cope with frustration. Lois Murphy observed that,

> High, as well as low, attention, body contact, and talking to the baby was not good for his development. In other words, a balance of attention with autonomy, of interaction with letting him alone part of the time, was related to the later coping capacity of the child.[1]

Caregivers who can respect the baby's need for autonomy seem to understand that protesting, and having the need to protest, is good. Babies need to learn to tolerate some frustration and to be able to delay having their needs met. Naturally the optimum degree of frustration varies with each individual (we will discuss this further in Chapter 9), but facing frustration and struggling to meet personal needs actually helps children develop the ability to cope with most situations they will face later on. In other words, the sensitive caregiver will not anticipate each and every need of the baby, will not always and instantly respond to every whimper, but will sometimes leave the baby alone to encourage the development of self-calming skills (which we will discuss in Chapter 9). These skills in turn expand into problem-solving skills. The caregiver's message is: "I believe that you can take care of yourself; when you can't, I am here to help you learn." When an infant begins to realize that some people around him will help him meet his needs and will support his efforts, he in turn will make efforts to understand the events in his world and become autonomous.

Think about your own attachment behaviors as an adult. What attachment behaviors do you show or have you shown? How does your attachment serve you?

Does being attached mean the same thing to you as being dependent? Can you be attached and still retain your autonomy (independence)?

Attachment and day care

The infant behaviors that are part of the process of attachment described at the beginning of this chapter become more complex over time. By eight or ten months infants react with fear to strangers and seem very anxious if separated from their special persons. They will begin to explore more, so long as one of the special persons is present. As in the case of Susan, the security in being able to touch home base seems necessary for facilitating further exploration.

Several very practical questions therefore arise: Is the reciprocal, responsive interaction that is so vital to the process of attachment possible outside the home and with someone other than the primary caregiver (who is usually, or very often, the mother)? What happens to the process of attachment when an infant leaves the home for substitute care before six months? Will early separation from the mother influence later personality development? To how many caregivers can infants comfortably be "attached?"

Evidence on the effects of day care on infant development is still sparse, and thus the best answer so far has to be, "it depends." It depends on what is happening at home. It depends on how parents feel about their role. (If parents feel good about themselves and each other and their reasons for seeking day care for their child, they are more apt to seek, within their means, settings that provide good care.) And it depends on the quality of the day care setting. Most of the research that does exist states that infant day care is not detrimental to development if caregivers are nurturant, responsive adults and if the quality of the care is exemplary.

Such information is not especially reassuring, since it is very hard to define and identify a "quality" setting, a "nurturing" adult, or "exemplary care." For instance, a low ratio of adults to infants and a "trained" caregiver both sound good, but do not guarantee "exemplary" care. Obviously there are no simple answers—though some of the implications of these issues were discussed in the chapters on caregiving and infant curriculum—and thus far research evidence is not strong enough to deal with all the questions we just raised concerning infant day care. It does seem clear that quality contact with a primary caregiver and the fostering of a reciprocal, mutually responsive series of interactions are ideal. The strongest implication coming from infancy research is that loving and learning are intertwined. As children experience consistently loving, respectful interactions, their learning about the world expands. We hope that in the next few years research will add much more to our understanding of how to make a better life for babies at home and in day care.

The effects of lack of attachment

Have you ever experienced trying to get close to someone who was indifferent, or being indifferent to someone trying to get close to you? As an adult you can usually choose to establish a relationship with someone or not. Infants, however, do not have that choice. If they are to thrive, it is *vital* that the process of attachment be provided for, even if it takes a great deal of time and effort.

So far we have focused on the ideal relationship that fosters the attachment process; the infant and the caregiver respond to each other in ways that bring mutual delight, as well as the care necessary for the infant. What about a relationship that is less than ideal?

Sometimes an infant's behaviors do not elicit delight or even care from an adult. Not only may the infant not have a set of pleasing behaviors, he may reject any snuggling or cooing behavior. In this case the adult must consciously provide opportunities for attachment to develop—continually trying to interact with and respond to the infant even though there is little immediate reward. The adult may have to initiate interactions if the infant does not.

Sometimes an attachment relationship is interrupted. Caregiver and baby may be separated for one reason or another, such as hospitalization, or delays can occur because of prematurity, changing foster homes, or early institutionalization.

Sometimes problems lie with the caregiver. For a variety of reasons an adult may be indifferent to the infant's attempts to get care or attention, ignore his cries for long periods, or handle him roughly. The infant's cuteness, smiles, and coos may bring no response at all. In this case the infant very likely will not give up. His desire for attachment is strong and he will keep trying, even though the response he gets may be an angry shout or a smack on the bottom. He would rather get a negative reaction from his caregiver than none at all. It is as if he is saying, "If I can't get your smiles and warmth, at least I'll get your tears and anger." Anything is better than nothing.

What happens if there is no attachment? A significant answer came from Harry Harlow, who learned something about attachment without even setting out to study it. He was interested in isolating rhesus monkeys so that they could live in a disease-free environment and not infect each other. He took 56 newborn monkeys and raised them in separate cages away from each other and their mothers. He was surprised to find that they grew to be very different adults from the rest of their species. They were unsocial, indifferent, and aggressive compared to other rhesus monkeys, who are normally social and cooperative. None of the monkeys raised in isolation mated.[2]

There are some implications here for child rearing. Although virtually no one attempts to raise a child in total isolation, it too frequently happens that children are raised without enough human physical contact, without opportunities for interaction, and without consistent treatment. This kind of deprivation occurs in some institutions. In such a situation the problems are multiple. Though the infants have contact with adults who feed and change them, the adults may vary from day to day and the infants may be unable to distinguish one from the other, or find that their attachment behavior when they are being cared for brings no consistent response. They find no one to call their own—no one whom they can influence. Eventually such children give up and no longer try to influence anyone. Furthermore, lacking not only attachment, but adequate physical contact, these infants are deprived of the variety of sensory input that comes with a healthy relationship. They become passive and noncomplaining, their development slows, they may eventually fail to thrive at all. Researchers believe that it is important for babies to have established a consistent attachment to at least one person before four to six months of age.[3]

The implications of attachment for adulthood

Obviously, any breakdown in the attachment process can be a cause for concern. But human beings are resilient, and early difficulties may be smoothed out if they are corrected and a warm, consistent environment is provided. A study spanning a 30-year period showed that a group of 13 children who spent their first two years in an orphanage, and were labeled retarded, grew up to be normal, self-supporting adults. After they were classified (early) as mentally retarded, they were sent to another institution, where they were cared for by a group of retarded girls who gave them mothering. This mothering apparently changed their lives. When compared 20 years later to a group who had remained in the orphanage, the "mothered" group showed significantly higher IQ's, were more successful in their educational experience, and were able to support themselves outside the institution.[4]

Throughout this chapter we have shown how attachment influences some aspects of infant development, but many questions about how the early attachment process influences later adult functioning have a long way to go to be clearly answered. Why do many people seem to grow older without growing up? How is attachment related to the adult personality? What are the differences between "normal adult functioning" and "optimal adult functioning?" Although we do not know the answers, there is no evidence that varying the attachment process is detrimental to development. The Kibbutzim in Israel, for example, have made a conscious attempt to change the pattern of the mother-infant attachment. Because a valued adult characteristic is to put the group first, early attachment to a single adult is not promoted. Instead, the Kibbutzim provide for early attachment to peers, supplemented with care from several adults.

Many people seem to understand the importance of the attachment process, yet they see the bond as a welded joint instead of an elastic thread. They interpret the concern for attachment to mean that the baby should be physically attached to the mother most of the time. In some cultures this approach is the normal one. In most cultures of modern America, however, the welded bond is a handicap to both mother and baby. The image of attachment as an elastic thread acknowledges that the baby is separate yet connected.

Our major point should be reiterated. A child may become attached to more than one adult at home, such as a parent and a long-term baby sitter, both parents, or parents and grandparents. Likewise, in a day care center infants may become attached to several people. The most important issue is not to whom the infant is attached, but whether the infant has the opportunity for attachment to develop and thus whether the care that fosters the attachment process is consistent and responsive.

Summary thought questions

1. Define "attachment."
   What infant behaviors foster attachment?
2. How do attachment behaviors change as the infant grows?
3. How are attachment and trust related?
4. Describe the kinds of interactions that build attachment.

5. What happens to development if no attachment is made or if adult-infant interactions are less than ideal?

Notes

1 Lois Murphy, "Later Outcomes of Early Infant and Mother Relationships," in L. J. Stone, et al., eds., *The Competent Infant* (New York: Basic Books, 1973), p. 112.

2 Harry Harlow, "The Nature of Love," *American Psychology,* 1958, **13**, pp. 59-60.

3 John Bowlby, *Attachment and Loss, Vol. I: Attachment* (London: Hogarth, 1969), p. 386.

4 H. M. Skeels, "Adult Status of Children with Contrasting Early Life Experiences." *Monographs of the Society of Research in Child Development,* 1966, **31**, 114.

Further reading

Bettleheim, Bruno. *The Children of the Dream.* New York: Macmillan, 1969.

Bowlby, John. *Child Care and the Growth of Love.* London: Penguin, 1953.

Bronfenbrenner, Uri. *Two Worlds of Childhood: U.S. and U.S.S.R.* New York: Basic Books, 1970.

Gerber, Magda, "Infants' Expression: The Art of Becoming." In *Conscious and Unconscious Expressive Art,* ed. I Jakab, *Psychiatry and Art,* Vol. 3, pp. 170-175. Basel: S. Karger, 1970.

Klaus, H., and Kennel, J. *Maternal-Infant Bonding.* St. Louis, Mo.: Mosby, 1976.

CHAPTER 7
The Development
of Perception
and Motor Skills

Infants can only indicate what they perceive by making some sort of muscular movements. Consequently we cannot learn much about infants' perception without taking into consideration their motor abilities. Researchers conclude that an infant "likes" certain sights because she reacts to them by moving or quieting. When the infant "likes" something, she becomes active, if she was still; if she is already actively moving around when something comes into view that she "likes," she settles down, quieting her muscles. Without these kinds of reactions we would have no idea what was perceived, how it was received, or indeed if anything was perceived at all.

The link between motor experience and sensory or perceptual awareness is strong. As infants move, they take in different sensory experiences. As they become aware of various perceptual differences, they move to accommodate to them. This interaction between movement experience and perceptual awareness is vital as infants begin to make sense of their world. In this chapter we examine perceptual or sensory abilities and motor skills, keeping in mind that they are always interacting and influencing each other.

Perceptual skills

We propose that you do an exercise to make you aware of your perceptions in preparation for reading about infants' perceptions. Try the following exercise. Two or more people can do it together, so long as everyone is silent.

Choose something you like the taste and smell of (a sprig of mint, a piece of apple) and take what you have chosen to a place where you can be alone and quiet (a dark room or even a closet).

- Block out all of your senses except smell and taste. Then pay attention to what you have brought along to smell and taste. Concentrate first on your sense of smell only; then on your sense of taste. When you have fully explored these, put the substance away. Notice how the sensation fades. When the flavor is gone, move on.

- Become aware of your body. Sense the places on your body where your clothes touch, where you feel pressure. Pay attention to these sensations. Change position and note the changes you feel.

- Be aware of your body in relation to the space it occupies. Feel the space around you. "Sense," without touching, where your body ends and the space begins. Explore the relationship between your body and this space. Try expanding and contracting your body; alter the space it takes up.

- Now move your attention from your whole body to your hands. Explore around you with your hands, noticing the textures and forms your fingers encounter. Pay attention only to what your fingertips feel.

- Move your focus from your hands to your ears. Pay attention to everything that is coming in through your ears. Now pick out the noise closest to you and listen to it carefully. Next, shift your attention to the noise that is farthest from you. Now see if you can concentrate on sounds coming from inside you. Finally, turn on all the noises at once and take them in without sorting them out.

- Now move your attention to your eyes. Open your eyes (or let light into the room). Look around. Focus on an object near you. See if you can make the object disappear by looking only at the spaces around it and between its parts. Concentrate on these negative spaces for a minute or so. Then take in more objects. Look at them carefully. Then concentrate on the space around and between them. Shift your focus from the space back to the objects and back to the space again. Try concentrating only on background, then on foreground, then on a single object. Let your eyes go out of focus.

- Come back to your normal perceptive state.

Now reflect on the order in which you experienced your senses. If you did the exercise, you went from perceiving through very localized physical contact (your taste buds) to generalized physical contact (your skin). Then you went on to perceive with two senses that extended beyond physical contact—hearing and seeing. With these you took in events or objects at a distance.

Infants learn to use their senses in much the same order. They first depend most on perceptions that are direct and physical—especially those that come in through their mouths. An infant's mouth is his main learning tool in the first months of life. As infants grow they learn to "extend" themselves by tuning in to the senses that bring information from a distance.

This ability to "tune in" to experience and concentrate on certain aspects of it allows an organizational process to develop. This process is neurological—it cannot be seen. But we can see infants adjust to their experiences. Even though all the senses are operating, initially infants do not realize that the information they receive from these senses has continuity. They cannot yet perceive the repetitiveness of events or interpret them. In a short time, however, connections between separate events are clarified. For example, a crying infant will calm down as she realizes that hearing a particular voice or seeing a particular face means that food or care is about to be given.

In the discussion that follows we will present current information about the infant's developing five senses. But it is interesting to speculate about possible other senses and whether infants may have many more sensory abilities than we retain as adults. Examine the following passage from *The Metaphoric Mind*, a book which argues that we have not five or six but twenty or more senses.

> Some human beings clearly detect minute changes in gravitational and magnetic fields. Others can detect the energy created by a flow of material in pipes, movement through soil, or electrostatic currents in the air. As adults these people are considered unique, mystical, or deviant in some other way. It may well be that these people have simply retained an awareness of senses they possessed as children.[4]

As time goes by and observational and technological skills improve, it will be interesting to see whether evidence is found to support this hypothesis.

As you examine the information that follows, ask yourself these questions: What does it mean to the parent or caregiver of an infant? How might it change my behavior as a caregiver? How should it influence the way I would design a setting for an infant at home or in a day care center?

Hearing   Newborns can hear at birth (and probably before). They can sense the direction from which sound comes as well as its frequency and duration. Researchers have found that sounds of 5 to 15 seconds seem to have the most effect on the infant's level of activity and heart rate (the two measures most frequently used to reflect an infant's awareness of a change in an event). If the sound lasts over several minutes the infant becomes less responsive.

Experiments have shown that infants only 20 weeks old can discriminate between the syllables "bah" and "gah." Listening to people's voices and noting differences seems to be an obvious early skill. The way infants react to sounds or any other sensory stimulation, however, depends a great deal on the situation in which they experience them. A loud or strange noise may be frightening, but the presence of a familiar, comforting caregiver transmits a sense of security and allows the infant to remain calm and open to learning.

With just this much information about early hearing abilities, what practical implications can you think of? Consider noise-making toys such as rattles and music boxes. Could there be too many sounds in an infant's environment? Do you think an infant should always be in a very quiet environment?

What would you do to help infants develop their hearing abilities?

Infants need the opportunity to experience a variety of sounds, and they need quiet times in order to appreciate the differences in sounds. If a music box is constantly making noise, for instance, the infant eventually stops listening because the sound is no longer interesting. Therefore, caregivers should be sure that mechanical toys and other noisemakers do not become substitutes for the human voice. Infants can determine a great deal from the inflection of a person's voice, and attending to the human voice and its inflections is the beginning of language development.

Smell and taste Less is known about smell than about the other senses. Researchers know that it is present at birth, but in a primitive form. Newborns respond to unpleasant strong odors such as ammonia or acetic acid by turning away but seem insensitive to odors that are fainter. An increase in breathing rate and activity level can be noted when odors are present in the air, and the greater the saturation of the odors, the greater the heart rate and level of activity.

Taste does not seem to be present at birth, but by two weeks the infant can distinguish between sweet and bitter, and prefers sweet. Salt taste is recognized soon after and will be accepted if the infant is hungry. A ten-day-old infant can show surprise if water is substituted for the expected milk, but there seems to be a correlation with whether the baby has been well fed: infants whose diet has been inadequate do not seem to notice taste differences rapidly.

Think about how these two senses, smell and taste, help developing infants understand their world. Might they contribute to their understanding of a familiar area or person? What else have you noted about these senses from your experiences with infants?

How have you seen an infant experience taste and smell. How do your senses of smell and taste serve you? Do they serve an infant the same way?

Touch Sensitivity to discomfort and pain increases rapidly after birth. Some parts of the body are more sensitive than others. The head, for example, is more sensitive than the arms and legs. Girls tend to be more sensitive to touch than boys, but individual babies vary, and some are more sensitive than others.

Tactile perception is correlated with motor abilities. As motor abilities increase, touch gives infants more and more information about the world. When babies develop from simply turning over to scooting, creeping, crawling, and finally walking, their tactile experiences expand a great deal. Words that have been repeated in front of them may finally acquire meaning, as the child holds the "fuzzy toy kitty" and cuddles the "soft blanket." Familiar objects seen from the crib take on new perspectives when they can be touched and examined from several angles.

How does your sense of touch serve you? Does it serve an infant in the same way? What guides would you offer a new parent concerning his baby's sense of touch?

Would you treat male and female infants differently because of some of this information?

Seeing The visual capabilities of adults and infants seem quite varied. More is known about sight than about the other senses, probably because all people depend so heavily on it. Infants can distinguish light and dark areas at birth. The pupillary reflex (the automatic narrowing of the pupil in bright light and widening in dim light) can be seen at birth, even in premature infants. Within a few hours infants are capable of visual pursuit. Their fixed focus seems to be about eight inches away. In other words, infants are equipped to see the mother's face while nursing.

Within a few weeks infants can discriminate among colors and prefer warm colors (red, orange, yellow) to cool ones (blue and green). Eye movements are somewhat erratic at first, but rapidly become more refined. By the end of the second month infants can focus both eyes to produce a single, though probably blurred, image. By the fourth month they can focus their eyes and see clearly. Their ability to see is then comparable to that of an adult.

Most newborns find all people and objects placed in front of them interesting, but during the first three months they may need to have cues that really hold their attention. Visual experiences that involve motion, sounds, sharp color contrast, and distinctive contours and patterns (especially black and white patterns) seem to be of most interest. Nevertheless, the experiment described below demonstrates that familiarity is at least as attention-attracting as vivid visual cues.

Four drawings were shown to a group of four-month-old boys (see Figure 7.1). The first drawing resembled a human face; the second was the outline of a face with an eye missing and lines and squiggles filling the outline at random. The third drawing was a face outline that was blank except for a nose; and the fourth had no facial features at all, only the outline filled with the same squiggles as the second drawing.

The babies paid the most attention to the first drawing, the most recognizable face, even though it was less complex than the drawings with squiggles. The second drawing was also second in the amount of attention it attracted, apparently because it was a face lacking only one eye.

Figure 7.1

The experimenters concluded that in this instance what interested the babies most was neither complexity nor amount of detail, but "faceness." Their general conclusion was that babies' attention is attracted to objects that look familiar. In different contexts, however, novelty is often quite as effective an attention-getter as familiarity, especially when it is combined with movement.[2]

What practical applications does this information on infants' visual abilities have? Infants need to be able to see interesting things. A variety of visual material encourages infants to move around in their world (something interesting to see becomes something interesting to reach for) and to understand their place in it. Too much visual stimulation, however, can lead to a situation we call the "circus effect." This encourages infants to become entertained observers rather than active participants. An entertained observer is quite different from a scientific observer. Entertained observers get hooked on a constant flow of novel visual stimulation. They get bored quickly and demand constant visual change. They may become television addicts. Because they experience such a strong assault on one sense (the visual), they ignore the fact that they are not actually involved physically or socially with the world around them. This eventual habit of observation and lack of involvement is detrimental to the development of a wide range of abilities.

How much should caregivers provide for infants to look at? What kinds of visuals? On what principles would you set up the visual environment of a day care setting?

Perception is an ongoing adaptive process. The perceptual equipment of the infant differs only in relatively minor ways from that of the adult, and then primarily during the early stages of development. By six months, infants probably perceive the world much the way adults do. Only their lack of experience and mature thinking abilities keep them from being able to interpret their perceptions.

Hard as it may be, it is important to try to take cues from infants themselves concerning how much stimulation of any sort is too much and when interesting experiences will be welcome. If an infant cries at certain things, it may be that too much is going on or that she is not yet ready to leave what she was paying attention to. If she is very quiet she may be concentrating on something in particular, or she may be "turned off" by too many events. When infants find their world interesting and are allowed to explore it at their own pace, they learn to entertain themselves in the process of discovery.

Motor skills

Without muscular coordination your perceptions (and your thoughts) would be locked inside (if, indeed, they would occur at all). Life as you know it is dependent

Figure 7.2
Reflexes at and after birth

At birth

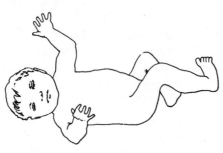

Moro reflex
(Startle reflex)

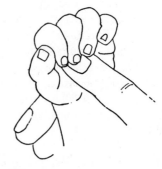

Palmar grasp

Tonic neck reflex

Rooting reflex

on your muscles. Without the muscles of your eyes you would see little, if anything. Without your hand muscles you could do little about what you did see. Without the intricate muscles of the throat, tongue, and other organs of speech your communication would be severely restricted. Without your heart muscles (or a substitute) you would have no life at all.

The infant's ability to use his muscles is quite different from yours, but the potential, obviously, is there. Infants are born with an internal blueprint for developing the basic skills and abilities that you as an adult possess, and they go right to work doing just that soon after birth. Within a year and a half or so they have learned most of the basic motor skills—sitting, walking, arm/hand coordination—that they will need throughout their lifetime. They spend the next years perfecting, expanding, and refining the original postures and movements that they learned early.

Reflexive movements Newborns can make few voluntary movements beyond the gross random movements of the arms and legs. Most of their first

After birth

Landau reflex

Reciprocal kicking

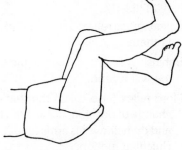

Parachute reflex

movements are reflexive; that is, the muscles react automatically in the presence of different kinds of stimuli. The refined and complex movements that they make are also reflexive in nature.

Reflexes serve several functions. Some, like blinking, swallowing, and clearing the face for breathing are protective. Others, such as kicking the legs alternately (reciprocal kicking), are precursors of later skills, in this case walking.

Pediatricians and other infant specialists pay attention to reflexes because they indicate brain growth. As the growth of the brain shifts from the brain stem to the cortex, reflexes change or disappear. Figure 7.2 illustrates some of the reflexes described below.

Reflexes present at birth   The reflexes we discuss below are the most visually obvious and the most often checked when infants are being examined by physicians. It can be helpful for parents and caregivers to realize that the early movements they notice are important signs of growth and that they will change or disappear as the infant matures.

Stepping: If you stand a newborn on his feet, he will respond to the pressure by stepping.

Palmar grasp reflex: The hands of a newborn curl tightly around any object placed in them.

Babinski reflex: If you stroke the sole of the foot, the toes will fan out, and the big toe will extend.

Moro reflex (also called the startle reflex): If a newborn is startled by a sudden change of position, noise, etc., he flings his arms out, with fingers spread wide, and then draws his arms (and, to a lesser extent, legs) back toward his body in a clutching motion.

Rooting and sucking: If you touch the cheek of a newborn he begins to search for a nipple with his mouth. When his mouth is touched he starts to suck.

Hand-to-mouth reflex: If a newborn's mouth and palm are touched, he puts his hand in his mouth. This is useful for clearing mucus in the early days, since when he sucks on his fist he can swallow easily.

Righting reflex (also called the china doll reflex): When the newborn is held upright, he tries to keep his head up and his eyes open.

Tonic neck reflex (sometimes called the fencer position): When the newborn's head is turned to one side, the arm on that side extends and the opposite arm flexes, making him look like a fencer. This reflex may eventually help the baby to use the sides of his body separately.

Swimming reflex: When the newborn is placed in water, he makes swimming motions.

Reflexes that appear after birth   Other reflexes make their appearance during the first few months. As the new reflexes appear, some of the original ones begin to disappear.

Reciprocal kicking (bicycling): If the infant is held out by an adult, he begins kicking his legs alternately. Usually this appears in the first month.

Neck righting: If the infant's head is turned, his body follows. This reflex begins to appear about the time the tonic neck reflex disappears.

Parachute reflex: If the infant begins to fall forward from an upright position, he tries to catch himself—arms go forward with hands outstretched. This reflex appears about the time the Moro reflex fades.

Landau reflex: If the baby is held under the stomach only, he extends his arms and legs. This extension, which indicates the strength of the back, is a precursor of walking. It is complete at about one year.

Not only is it interesting to see how reflexes serve as the basis for later movement, it is useful for caregivers to know what reflexes indicate about infants' behavior and development. For instance, it is sometimes useful to know that a baby has not chosen to move in a certain way, for example, rooting before he starts to suck, but that he or she has to do so.

Furthermore, the appearance of certain reflexes and the absence of others can indicate certain differences in development, as can reflexes that remain instead of fading. This aspect of development is well understood.[3] When parents or caregivers notice that a baby is showing what seems to be inappropriate reflexive behavior, they may want to discuss what they have noticed with a doctor.

Chapter 7
The
Development of
Perception and
Motor Skills

101

Voluntary movements Eventually—at about eight months—infants make motions that are not automatic, but voluntary. These movements are generally divided into two broad types: gross motor, having to do with large muscles and big movements, and fine motor, having to do with small muscles and more delicate movements.

Gross motor development Various large muscles contribute to the infant's ability to move in two directions: *up* (to an upright position) and *around* (on a horizontal plane). The two are intertwined, as the child needs to get up to move around and needs to move around to get up. Little by little babies gain control over these muscles. The first muscles to develop are those that control movements of the head. As babies perfect the skills involved in turning the head from side to side and lifting it up, they strengthen the shoulder muscles. As they begin to move around and squirm, lifting their arms and legs, they develop the trunk muscles. All this preparation is for turning over, just as turning over is preparation for (i.e., strengthens the muscles necessary for) sitting up. A child will learn to come to a sitting position without ever having been propped up. The ability to sit comes from developing the muscles prerequisite to the upright position. The infant gets ready to sit by learning to move his head and by turning over. The building of the muscle systems is vital—practice at sitting is not.

A general principle involved in motor development is that stability is the means to mobility. Infants cannot move until they gain a good solid base from which to move—whether the movement is vertical, as in sitting or standing, or horizontal, as in crawling or walking. We saw this same principle in action on the psychological level in Chapter 6—from psychological stability (trust in attachment) comes psychological as well as physical mobility (exploration). The plan for developing muscular stability is a part of the makeup of the infant—just as is the plan for mobility. Nobody has to "teach" either sitting or walking—when babies have gone through the necessary muscle development, they will be able to sit and walk.

Figure 7.3 shows the major milestones of gross motor development. Use it with caution. Such charts are based on averages, and no individual baby is average. The sequence of motor development is mostly standard, but within it lies a good deal of room for individual variation in timing and style.

To help you apply some of the information we have presented here to caregiving situations, we offer the following suggestions:

- Try to keep children in the position in which they are freest and least helpless during their waking hours. Do not, for instance, keep a child hour after hour in an infant seat, jump chair, swing, high chair, or car seat.
- Don't try to hurry development. Babies get ready for the next stage by doing

Figure 7.3
Gross motor development milestones:
birth to thirty months

Raises self by
arms in prone position
2.1 months
(range 0.7 – 5 months)

Prewalking progression
7.1 months
(range 5 – 11 months)

Pulls to sit
7.3 months
(range 6 – 8 months)

Pulls up on furniture
8.6 months
(range 6 – 12 months)

Stands alone
11 months
(range 9 – 16 months)

Walks alone
11.7 months
(range 9 – 17 months)

Walks backward
14.6 months
(range 11--20 months)

Jumps off floor
23.4 months
(range 17 – 30 months)

Source·
Adapted by permission from the Bayley Scales of Infant Development. The Psychological Corp., 1969
New York.

thoroughly whatever it is they are doing in the present stage. You cannot teach babies to roll over or walk. They reach each milestone only when they are ready.

Chapter 7
The
Development of
Perception and
Motor Skills
103

- Don't put babies into positions they cannot get into by themselves. The process of getting into a position is more important than being in the position—it is the process that promotes development.

- Don't shield babies from all physical stress. The body needs a certain amount of stress to grow. Reasonable—optimum—stress stimulates growth, increases motivation, and strengthens the body as well as the psyche.[4]

As we said in Part I, we encourage caregivers and parents to *facilitate* development rather than push it. Because we live in a "hurry-up" culture, some people are most anxious for babies to reach milestones "on time," or even *"early."* We suggest that "in time" is a better motto for milestones than "on time." Instead of worrying about *what* infants are doing (and whether or not they are on time), we should worry about *how well* they are doing whatever it is they are doing. The quality of movement is more important than whether or not infants are doing what they are "supposed" to do. The questions to ask yourself are, "How do they use the skills they have?" and "How are they progressing?" With these two concerns in mind you will not have to be so concerned about where they fit on the chart.

Now take time to list the practical ways you can think of to facilitate freedom of movement. Consider such things as clothes, shoes, position (lying on front or back), and infant carriers and harnesses. Write here some ways to facilitate freedom of movement.

Did you find facilitating freedom of movement was sometimes in conflict with social convention or convenience? Caregiving is often a matter of setting priorities; for example, is it more important for a child to be dressed in cute clothes or to be able to move freely?

Fine motor development   Let us look now at the development of fine motor control. The small muscles that a baby gradually gains control of include the muscles of the eyes, mouth, speech organs, rectum, hands, and fingers. We will look closely at one set—the muscles of the hands and fingers—and the development of manipulative skills. We have chosen to examine this skill in particular because so many tasks in our daily lives involve the use of the hands and fingers.

The sequence in which infants learn to manipulate objects precisely shows how complex this ability is. Figure 7.4 illustrates the developmental sequence. At first newborns generally hold their hands in tight fists (although this may be changing with new so-called gentle birth procedures). They hold on to any object put into their hands, gripping so tightly that they can, if held up, support their own weight. But they have no control over their grasp and cannot let go at will. (What does this imply about putting a rattle in an infant's hand?) At some time before six months (usually a little over two and a half months) the tight fists relax, and the hands remain open most of the time.

During the first three months more of the hand and arm movements become voluntary. Infants begin to reach for objects, first with their eyes, then with open hands. By around three and a half months they can often close on an object within reach. They may also begin to play with their own hands about this same time. The way they grasp at first is distinctive: they use all the fingers together as if they had a mitten on, drawing objects into the palm of the hand. This motion is called the "palmar grasp." Although at this stage the palmar grasp is a voluntary movement, it comes from the earlier palmar grasp reflex present at birth. After learning to pick up objects with one hand, infants soon begin to pass them back and forth between the two hands. By the sixth month they have begun trying to use thumb and forefinger in what is called a "pincer grasp." They can then manipulate objects with more skill and a variety of motions.

By about the ninth month infants have perfected the pincer grasp and can pick up small objects with great adeptness. Playing with the hands—picking up and dropping objects for a helpful adult to retrieve and playing patticake—provides pleasure. The dropping game shows infants' joy in and awareness of now being able to let go. By the ninth month infants may also be using their forefingers alone, poking, hooking, and probing. Eventually they can differentiate the uses of the hands and can then do two different activities at once, for example, holding something with one hand and maneuvering with the other. By eleven months, infants can hold crayons and mark on available surfaces, and they can probably get a spoon to their mouths. By a year the variety of movements has come a long way from the compulsive grasping that was present at birth. Infants can take covers off objects, undress themselves to some degree, take one thing out of another, and take things apart and move them around. They continue to expand

Figure 7.4
Fine motor development:
manipulative skills, birth to twenty-one months

Chapter 7
The
Development of
Perception and
Motor Skills

105

Grasps and holds ring
.8 months
(range .3−3 months)

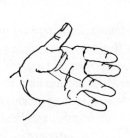

Hands predominantly
open and relaxed
2.7 months
(range .7−6 months)

Reaches for dangling ring
3.1 months
(range 1−5 months)

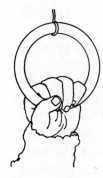

Closes on dangling ring
3.8 months
(range 2−6 months)

Fingers hand in play
3.2 months
(range 1−6 months)

Palmar grasp
3.7 months
(range 2−7 months)

Neat pincer grasp
8.9 months
(range 7−12 months)

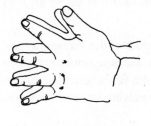

Patticake (Midline skills)
9.7 months
(range 7−15 months)

Scribbles spontaneously
14 months
(range 10−21 months)

Source:
Adapted by permission from the Bayley Scales of Infant Development The Psychological Corp., 1969.
New York).

their manipulative skills, refining their movements and perfecting them. From here on individuals vary greatly.

We will end this chapter by showing you an inside and an outside view of the "activity" of two infants, both about ten months old.

We focus first on Bruce, a healthy-looking boy with a medium build and padded cheeks and tummy. Right now he is sitting quietly in the living room of a small apartment. The door is open and a gentle breeze comes in through the screen. Although there are toys around him, Bruce is intently watching a piece of paper that the breeze keeps lifting gently off the rug. We tune in on the monologue that might be running through Bruce's head if he could talk. We must keep in mind, however, that we are only "hearing" perceptions that can be put into words. There may be other things going on inside him for which there are no words.

Bruce: (There goes that paper again. First the corner near me goes up in the air, then the one on the other side. Each time that happens I feel a puff of air on one arm, leg, and cheek. How interesting! There it goes again! I wonder what will happen if I turn the paper around. There! Oh, it moves differently now. I still feel the same puff on me, but the paper doesn't act the same. That's interesting! Oh, yes—another interesting thing is that shape that's moving on the wall. I don't know what it is, but I see that its movements match the paper's. It doesn't look like the paper at all, but I feel some kind of sameness about it. I like to look at it. It keeps changing. I like to look at the moving shape, then at the paper, and feel the air on my skin at the same time. I also notice some nice smells. One is coming in on the air. The others are coming from the kitchen. I like those smells. When I pay attention I can hear noises too. There is a faint flapping sound that goes along with the air. And best of all there's my mother's voice talking in the kitchen. She isn't talking to me, but I like to hear that sound anyway. In fact I think I'll go watch her awhile.)

Bruce crawls slowly to the door of the kitchen, where he settles back into a comfortable sitting position. He is so unobtrusive that no one notices he is there. We leave the scene with Bruce watching the action in the kitchen with much interest, emotional involvement, and contentment.

Now we find ourselves in another living room. It is empty of people, though some toys are scattered here and there. We hear a sound from beyond a doorway. Bump, bump, bump. Into view comes Bret, crawling at a fast pace. Dragging along behind him, upside down, is a little wagon caught by its string to one of his legs. Bret pauses for a moment, shoves at the wagon, kicks his leg free, and continues forward. Here is the monologue going on inside him:

Chapter 7
The
Development of
Perception and
Motor Skills

107

Bret: (That's better. It was hard to move with that thing on my leg. Now I need something to put in it. Let's see what's here! Oh, there's a ball right over there—I'll just whip over and get it. There we are! I wonder if I can get it in the wagon from here. Might as well try. Ooops—missed! I'll just crawl over and get it. These other toys are right in my way—I'll just shove them over so I can get through. Here's the ball now. I'll crawl back to the wagon and put it in. Hmm, it's harder to crawl with the ball in my hand. Never mind—skip the crawling—I'd rather get up on that chair. Oh, it's hard to pull myself up with this ball in my hand. That's okay, I'll put it down when I get on top—no I won't, I'll throw it when I get on top. There, I'm up. That's it—might as well get down. Hey, where's Mommy? I'd like to crawl up on her lap right now. I'll listen a minute and see if I can hear where she is—oh, never mind—I'll just go look. Uh, oh, it's hard to get down—might as well get rid of this ball—look how it bounces when I drop it. There it goes—good-bye ball! Well, I'm down—now all I have to do is find Mommy. There's that wagon again—might as well shove it out of the way.)

We follow Bret out of the living room into the kitchen, where he goes straight to his mother, who is sitting on a stool. He grabs her leg, makes his way up like a monkey almost before she can offer to help. She starts to settle him on her lap, but before she can finish he is already on his way back down to the floor. As we leave the scene Bret is heading out another door.

These two scenes showed two little boys behaving differently and experiencing very different things in much the same circumstances. Although caregivers cannot know what infants perceive (that is, cannot read their minds, as we did in the two scenes), they can see differences in behavior. They may worry about less active infants because they cannot know what is going on inside them. But they should remember that the quiet, contemplative infant may well be quite busy taking in and sorting out sensory perceptions. This inner activity does not show, except as rather passive behavior. Since passive infants may take longer to acquire motor skills than more active, less contemplative ones, and since development is most often measured by motor skills (we do not have clear perceptual milestones), a quiet infant may be wrongly labeled "behind" or "slow." These scenes showed us that each infant has a unique way of using his perceptual and motor abilities to explore and understand his world. Even children similar in development may prefer to use the same skills in different ways.

Summary thought questions

1. Discuss the relationship between motor development and perceptual (sensory) development.
2. Reflect on what you have learned from this chapter concerning the development of one particular sense (hearing, taste, smell, touch, sight). How

might it influence the way you would interact with an infant?

3. Why are reflexes important? Describe at least six reflexes that are present during the first year.

4. Discuss the pros and cons of charts showing typical development.

5. How would you foster (not force) motor development?

Notes

1 Robert Samples, *The Metaphoric Mind* (Menlo Park, Ca.: Addison-Wesley, 1976), p. 95.

2 R. A. Haff and R. Q. Bell, "Facial Dimension in Visual Discrimination of Human Infants," *Child Development,* 1976, **38,** 895.

3 Una Haynes, *A Developmental Approach to Casefinding,* (Public Health Service Publication, #2017, 1967), pp. 14–27.

4 Seymore Levine, "Stimulation in Infancy," *Scientific American,* May 1960, **436,** 624.

Further reading

Gordon, Ira. *The Infant Experience.* Columbus, Ohio: Charles E. Merrill, 1975.

Bowers, T.G.R. *Development in Infancy.* San Francisco: W. H. Freeman, 1974.

Pikler, Emmi. "Data on Gross Motor Development." *Early Childhood Development and Care,* 1972, **1**.

CHAPTER 8
The Development of Knowing and Language

For an individual to understand and know the environment, a complex process of coordinating external and internal sensations must develop. Initially experience is perceived directly with the senses. For a person to become capable and acquire the ability to comprehend this sensory information, he must be able to distinguish between the familiar and the unknown, to consider, to formulate, to reason, and to imagine. This process of experiencing and clarifying the environment is what we will call the development of knowing.

How do infants develop knowing and understanding? Because part of this process is internal, certain assumptions concerning knowing must be inferred by observing obvious physical movements. Infants begin by exploring the world with their bodies. What is taken in through their senses becomes internalized and is displayed in their physical movements. Through such simple acts as mouthing, grasping, and reaching, infants gather vital information. You can see infants practicing these acts, repeating them over and over. Rather quickly they refine them. For example, when a newborn first brings her mouth toward a nipple, the mouth opens wide and ready. With only a few trials she learns just what size opening the nipple requires and adjusts her mouth accordingly in anticipation of what will go into it. She has refined a simple action. Soon she will judge how far to reach and what shape her fingers must take to pick up a cup or a toy. Much later, as an adult, she may refine her actions further in order to reach without looking and strike a particular chord on the piano. All these muscular refinements had their beginnings in that tiny mouth adjusting itself to the appropriate size for the nipple.

In this chapter the process of knowing will be viewed from two perspectives: the sensory-motor experience and the intuitive experience. The sensory-motor experience is to a large degree observable, the intuitive experience is not. Because the former experience is apparent, more material concerning its development is available.

This knowing process expands to incorporate language abilities. As the young child experiences her world through her senses and her body, her need for labels to categorize and remember these experiences develops. Once she attains labels for experience, she has increased her ability to communicate her desires and accomplishments. This expanded ability to communicate and store information opens up the young child to additional opportunities for understanding her world.

Knowing and language are linked to each other in the process of development. Exploring this link is a major objective of this chapter.

The sensory-motor experience of knowing

The coordination of the information from the senses and from the body is the basic definition of the sensory-motor experience. Babies turn their bodies toward the lights and sounds they have perceived. They grasp, suck, and cry. At first many of these acts are reflexive, and their consequences are accidental. A little arm swipes at a blanket or a toy, and it moves. A head turns to free the face from a corner of a blanket that has fallen over it. Soon, however, babies learn to make adjustments in their behavior. They begin to act more purposefully. They learn, for example, that sucking on a rattle may be interesting, but it is only sucking on the breast or bottle that satisfies hunger. Along with practicing movements, they begin to combine them. For instance, they begin to suck and look at the same time. They learn to bring their hands to their mouths and suck on them. They begin to touch their hands together and look at their fingers. They gradually begin to watch their hands as they touch objects and bring them to their mouths. These abilities become combined and coordinated—seeing and reaching for the same object, then grasping and sucking the same object. This happens as babies come to recognize cause and effect. These physical movements that lead toward understanding and knowing can be diagrammed as follows:

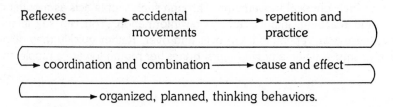

Reflexes ⟶ accidental movements ⟶ repetition and practice ⟶ coordination and combination ⟶ cause and effect ⟶ organized, planned, thinking behaviors.

Chapter 8
The
Development of
Knowing and
Language

111

Gradually babies come to know that they can control the interaction between themselves and objects. They like this new piece of knowledge and they keep testing it out. They want to repeat interesting activities. Through this testing, babies come to know that shaking a rattle produces a sound, but shaking a spoon does not. They soon learn, however, that banging a spoon will make a noise . . . and they like that and keep doing it!

When a baby is practicing and combining these first actions, he is in love with his own body—fascinated by what he is feeling and doing. Eventually that fascination moves from his own body to the effects of his actions on the environment. He gets interested in what happens when he shoves his arm out and hits a toy. You can see this same progression of development a bit later in preschool art. At first the child is most intersted in what it feels like when he scribbles or scrubs with a paint brush on paper. Later he starts looking at the product of his action—the drawing or the painting. A new understanding develops with this shift or focus from self to environment, from action to consequences. The baby begins to realize that he and the objects in his world are separate.

Knowing that he is in a world full of objects and part of it, but not the whole of it, is a great step forward in understanding for the infant. Along with this awareness comes some other abilities: the ability to anticipate where an object will be when he drops it; the ability to remember an action after a short interruption; and the ability to predict. For example, watch a child 18 months of age who has had experience with a ball. He may roll the ball off a table and turn his head to the place where the ball will land. Or if the ball rolls under a chair, he may go find a stick and then come back with it to push the ball from under the chair. Or he may roll the ball toward a hole and run to the hole to watch the ball rolling into it.

Nevertheless, the infant's idea of objects differs greatly from that of adults. He only acknowledges the existence of things that he can see, touch, or otherwise know with his senses. When you hide his favorite toy, he does not look for it because he believes it no longer exists. If you bring it out of hiding, for him it has been recreated. This understanding of the world makes a game of peek-a-boo extremely exciting. What power—to create and uncreate a person in an instant. No wonder peek-a-boo is a game with universal fascination.

At about one year of age a child begins to think in a more sophisticated way and to use tools. Give him a stick and he will use it to pull an out-of-reach toy to himself. Give him a string with something he wants at the end and he knows just what to do. Give him the problem of getting a stick into a play pen and he will discover that he must hold it vertically to draw it through the bars. Furthermore, novelty becomes an end in itself. The child will deliberately manipulate the environment to find out what happens.

The next step in the development of understanding comes when the infant can find solutions mentally. After enough experience using his sense perceptions and his muscles, he can begin to think of ways of acting and try them out in his head before putting them into action. He can predict. He can think of past events (or objects that are not present) and of events that could happen. You can see that he is using mental images and connecting thoughts to experiences and objects that are not present. Watch him throw an imaginary ball. Or see him contemplate the solution to a problem before he begins to tackle it.

Although anyone who has spent much time around an infant has seen understanding unfold, it is not as easy to talk about what is happening as it is to see and enjoy it. A man who has done much toward putting into words how a child develops knowing and understanding is Jean Piaget. He has defined four stages that lead to logical and abstract thought.[1] The first stage, consisting of six phases covering about the first two years, he calls the "sensorimotor" stage. This name, which means the coordination of sense perception and muscle movements, is appropriate since that coordination is the beginning of thinking. We have just described what happens during this stage. It can be summarized as follows:

1. Reflexes, simple inborn behaviors (crying, sucking, grasping)	1 month
2. Repeats and combines simple behaviors (reaching, grasping, and sucking on an object)	1-4 months
3. Repeats behaviors because something happens— produces an effect (shaking a rattle to hear a noise)	4-8 months
4. Plans (intention) a movement to have something happen (pulls a string to bring a toy closer)	8-12 months
5. Experiments with known things in order to create new events (a ball rolled off the table will bounce, what will a book do?)	12-18 months
6. Imagines events and solves problems, uses words (pretends to throw ball and calls to parent "here come ball")	18-24 months

Let us take a look at the behavior of three babies in view of what you have just read. See if you can determine approximately which "phase" each of these babies might be in. What do the behaviors tell you? Do you see overlapping behaviors—behaviors that might belong to two phases?

The first baby lies alone in a crib on his back. He is just waking up. As he wakes he stretches and accidently touches a bell hanging on a cradle gym stretched across the crib. He startles at the sound and looks toward the bell. He lies still, glancing at the bell now and then. Just as you are about to tire of watching because nothing is happening, he throws out his arms for no apparent reason. The bell rings again. He again startles and has a look of surprise on his face. You can almost hear his question, "Who did that?" He looks at the bell, looks around, and looks at the bell again. Then he lies still. A few moments later his arms come up and out again, this time tentatively waving. He misses the bell. Nothing happens. He lies still again. He repeats the action—again tentatively. This time his hand passes in front of his eyes and a spark of interest comes over his face. He looks intently at his hand and you can almost hear him saying, "What's that thing? Where did it come from?" He moves his fingers and delight comes into his eyes. "Hey, it works!'' he seems to say. His arms continue to wave, taking the fascinating fingers out of his line of vision. He breezes by the bell causing it to make just a whisper of a sound. His eyes search for the source of the sound. As we move back from him we are aware that the occasional waving of his arms continues. From a distance it appears as if very little is happening. All we can see is a baby lying rather quietly in his crib moving his arms now and then. But we have just watched closely enough to know that understanding is in progress and we tiptoe out as if there were a "do not disturb" sign on the door.

Chapter 8
The
Development of
Knowing and
Language

113

What phase do you think this infant could be experiencing?

Why? What behaviors tell you?

Are there any overlapping behaviors?

The baby we see now is sitting in the middle of a rug with several toys beside her and other toys on a low shelf nearby. She has a rubber toy in her hand and is banging it up and down on the floor, giggling at the squeaks issuing forth. The toy bounces across the rug as she lets go, and she crawls happily after it. She stops to explore a string with a bead on the end of it, then moves on after the rubber toy. She bounces it several more times before throwing it down, this time ignoring it as it bounces away. She returns to the string. She ignores the interesting bead on the end, but glances to see where the other end is. The string disappears into a pile of toys on the lowest shelf at the edge of the rug. She expectantly pulls the string and laughs delightedly when the pile of toys crashes down and a toy train emerges, attached to the other end of the string. She reaches out and pushes the train back—then pulls the string again. She laughs and claps delightedly. Then she catches sight of a bright red ball that has rolled out from the pile of toys that fell off the shelf. She crawls over to it and begins to smack it with her hand, making noises while doing so. She seems to expect the ball to move. When it doesn't, she tries again with more force. The ball moves slightly and she moves after it. She is getting more and more excited, and as she approaches the ball, one hand accidently swipes it so that it rolls some distance and disappears under a bed in the corner of the room. She watches it roll, starts after it, but stops when it disappears. Looking puzzled, she crawls over to the edge of the bed but does not lift up the bedspread to check under the bed. She looks a little disappointed, but then crawls back to the rug and the squeaky rubber toy. As the scene closes she is once again banging the toy against the floor and laughing at the noise it makes.

What phase do you think this infant could be experiencing?

Why? What behaviors tell you?

Are there any overlapping behaviors?

The third scene opens with a baby holding an empty pitcher in his hand. He goes over to a box of toys, reaches into the box, and brings out a small plastic bowl, an egg carton, and the lid to a peanut butter jar. He sets these in a row on a low table and pretends to pour something in them from his pitcher. He is careful in his actions and methodically fills each container, including each compartment of the egg carton. Then, seemingly satisfied that the task is done, he tosses the pitcher across the room with a joyous shout. He starts across the room in another direction, when he notices a plant standing on a table. He immediately runs over to where he threw the pitcher, rummaging through a pile of dolls and blankets where it landed until he finds it. He carries the pitcher over to the plant and carefully "waters" it. Then once again he tosses the pitcher away and picks up a doll. He scolds the doll, bangs it on the floor several times, wraps it in a blanket, then lovingly puts it to bed in the box of toys. As he bends over the box he spies a picture book on fire engines. He looks at the pictures for a moment, then puts the book on his head and races around the room screaming in what seems to be an imitation of a siren. As he passes by the toy box he stops to rummage around. He drags out a rather worn looking fire truck, which he proceeds to push around on the floor. He stops, looks at the holes on the truck where the little firefighters are supposed to sit. No little firefighters are visible anywhere. He pauses for a moment, then moves back to the pile of dolls, where he rummages around. He comes out empty handed and stands looking around the room. Suddenly he starts toward something—the pitcher. He grabs the pitcher and as the scene ends he is sitting by the fire truck carefully filling each hole—not with toy firefighters but with whatever mysterious substance the pitcher contains.

What phase do you think this infant could be experiencing?

Chapter 8
The
Development of
Knowing and
Language

115

Why? What behaviors tell you?

Are there any overlapping behaviors?

In thinking about these scenes we can only infer from their physical behaviors what the babies are understanding and thinking. As yet we know very little about their internal, unobservable processes.

The intuitive experience of knowing

We view thinking and knowing as a logical and rational activity and tend to ignore the potential ability to understand intuitively or emotionally. Initially in this chapter we defined knowing as a process of coordinating external and internal experience in order to "make sense" or understand the world. The sensory-motor experience, the process of combining accidental movements and practicing them and eventually recognizing cause and effect and prediction, may be considered a logical and rational process. It takes about two years for this process to mature. Might there be an intuitive process maturing simultaneously with this logical process? Might there be abilities present immediately in the infant that allow a total taking in of experience and unspecialized, limitless interpretation of the environment?

To what extent an infant understands intuitively, we do not know. The sorting out process that might be considered intuitive, and therefore without "formal logic," allows infants to experience no restriction in their sensory and motor involvement. While we are busy labeling their behaviors as initially accidental, then coordinated and combined, and so forth, they are perhaps experiencing all parts (internal and external) working together in an organized way that we cannot perceive. When they move, touch, taste, see, and experience, can we assume that no immediate individual interpretation is in progress?

This self-initiated exploration that contributes to knowing has been examined particularly by Robert Samples. His work provides a thought-provoking balance to the scientific work of Piaget. In the following quote, Samples comments on the totality of experience:

The sensorimotor repertoire has as its basic quality the quality of invention. Children in the first two years of life are inventing the whole universe that they perceive. . . . From the crib children are totally immersed in sensing all things. The clatter in the kitchen, the warm cooing sounds from parents, the feelings they get from different colors, the warmth, the cold, the feeling of liquids going into their bodies, the feeling of liquids coming out . . . all are of equal importance. Some even suggest that it is not an optical quandary facing children in the first few weeks of birth when they have trouble focusing —it may be a super sensory one. Newborn and early infants probably see the auras of energy associated with our bodies . . . a phenomenon we confuse with their eyes being "out of focus."[2]

The point we want to make is that sensory-motor experience and intuitive experience work together in the developing process of knowing. Neither one can stand alone and fully explain how an individual thinks and understands.

Let us look once again at a child experiencing her surroundings. Try to imagine what this child could be thinking. Let yourself see the world as she sees it and involve yourself in the total experience.

A small hand is filled with sand that is flowing out through the tiny fingers. The hand goes to the mouth of a baby girl sitting at the edge of a small sandbox. She tastes gingerly and screws up her face as her tongue and lips come in contact with the sand. She spits out the grains that managed to get inside, empties the rest of the sand on the ground, and reaches for another handful. As she does so she spies a spoon and plastic container on the other side of the sandbox. She crawls over, intent on reaching these items, when a leaf falls in her path from a branch overhead. She stops in wonder. She plops herself back into a sitting position and reaches enthusiastically for the leaf. She intently explores the leaf—looking at it as it lies in her hand, tasting it with relish as the end tickles her nose. As the scene fades she is busy crumpling and crushing it, apparently delighted at both the noise and the feel of the experience.

You may have noticed that the child is easily distracted from her original purpose. Yet at the same time we see complete absorption in the experience at hand, even though she just happened upon it. Is it that she is easily distracted, or that she is satisfied with the totality of the events in the world?

How would you compare this scene with the three in the previous section on sensory-motor experience?

You have already seen that infants are competent processors of information. As soon as they begin to remember simple experiences long enough to repeat them and then coordinate and combine them, they are ready to link language and knowing.

Language is more than communication with words. During the first year, infants are involved in the process of organizing experience in order to understand events. They use sensory-motor and intuitive information. Watch a child under one year, or reread the four scenes in this chapter. Note the developing mental abilities: memory, in order to repeat activities; organization, in order to coordinate and combine particular activities; and prediction, knowing that an object still exists even though it is out of sight. These developing mental abilities indicate the roots of language. Language is more than the utterance of the first word. It is the complicated system of organization that allows individuals to label experience, store information, categorize it, abstract from it, and reason with it. It is a lifelong process and it begins as soon as infants seek sensory-motor coordination. Language and knowing are interwoven in their development.

In the next section we will examine the foundations of language development, language styles, and some guidelines for fostering language development.

Chapter 8
The
Development of
Knowing and
Language

117

Learning to verbalize: Expressive language

Suppose you observed a child who was just beginning to talk and you wrote down exactly what the child "said." You might have a paper that looked something like this:

Words said:
mmm mm   ooo   milk
mimimimimi   burr burr
burr   burr
ooooo   milk
eeeeeeee   uh uh uh   milk

What does it mean? Without the context it is hard to know. But a description of the whole scene would clarify for you what the child was communicating.

A father holds out a cup to his young son seated at a low table. "Do you want a drink of milk?" he asks. The child answers, "MMMMMMMM, OOOOO, milk" and reaches for the cup. The father pours a small amount of milk into the cup. The child lifts it to his lips and drinks a sip. Then he says, "mimimimimimi, burr, burr" into the cup, delighted in the effect of the movement of his lips on the milk. Milk splashes onto his face. The father turns to the sink for a washcloth. While his back is turned, the child sets the cup down and it tips over, making a puddle on the table. "Oooooooo, milk," says the child. The father turns around, sees what has happened, grabs a sponge, and moves quickly to the table, washcloth in one hand, sponge in the other. Squeals of delight accompany the table cleaning and squeals of protest accompany the face cleaning. When all is in order again, the father reaches for the milk carton and asks, "Do you want more milk?" The child answers, "Milk," with a vigorous shake of his head, shoving the cup away from him.

The child conveyed a variety of meanings through a single word (and a few other sounds). In a short time this same scene might include this verbal sequence:

"Me milk," (meaning, "Yes, please, I'd like some milk.")

"Daddy milk spilled" (Meaning, "Hey, Dad somebody spilled the milk.")

"Me no." (Meaning, "No thank you, I don't want any more milk.")

In several months this same child will put together longer phrases:

"Give me milk."

"Oh, oh, Daddy. Me spilled milk."

"Me no want more."

Without ever being "corrected" this child will eventually (probably by the second year) say:

"I want some milk."

"Daddy, I spilled the milk."

"I don't want any more."

This child obviously can understand the events in his environment. He can label these experiences and use words. Many adults interpret these first words as the beginning of language. Actually, as we will see, language was developing in the first few weeks of the child's life.

Foundations of language: Receptive qualities

As their early cries and vocalizations are responded to, infants learn to refine them, eventually sending more specialized vocal signals. The more they know that their signals or messages are received, the more skilled they become in sending them. From their partnership with a caregiver they learn to convey a variety of feelings—hunger, discomfort, anger, pleasure—distinctively. The key to infants' beginning to connect sounds with meaning is the caregiver's responsiveness. If no one responded to the initial cries and vocalizations made by infants, there would be no reason for infants to strive to make signals.

With their partner or caregiver, infants also share their pleasure in making sounds. They come to associate language with a social occasion. As they coo and babble, they find that they are responded to and in turn respond to and imitate their partner. They also become aware of certain pleasing rhythms. At times these rhythms are soothing and enjoyable all by themselves, without connections at all. These times come about especially when they are sung to or read to, or when they are talked to in a soothing way.

Within several months infants begin to notice that their partners use some patterns of sounds more than others, and eventually they begin to make connections between sounds or sound patterns and events or objects. They notice, for example, that their story books have the same sounds with the same pictures. They notice that whenever their partners change their diapers, they hear some of

Chapter 8
The
Development of
Knowing and
Language

119

the same sounds. They notice also that they are listened to. They make sounds, they are answered with sounds, and then they make more sounds. There are also times of silence so that the sounds have a chance to sink in. (Infants are well aware of how confused they get when there is a clutter of sounds that do not stop and do not give them a chance to respond. During these times, they retreat into themselves and shut out all sounds.)

The actual moment a child utters his first word and enters the period of expressive language may be quite a surprise to the adult who is present. One day an infant finds the cookie jar on the table in the kitchen. He wants a cookie, so he reaches out to his partner with one hand and puts the other hand on the top of the cookie jar, and says the sound that he has heard many times, "cooo key." He is surprised by the reaction he gets—such a flutter and flurry of smiles, hugs, and pats, and then a cookie is placed in his hand. He smiles back and says his new word two or three more times. Later that day he repeats his performance for a neighbor. This (at about 12 months of age) is the beginning of verbalization.

From then on the infant does not just take in words (receptive language), he starts putting them out too (expressive language). He notices that whenever he says a single word his partner responds in a way that usually tells him his meaning was conveyed. He becomes more and more aware of the nature of the responses he is receiving. He likes a response that is meaningful, that relates to what he is doing and moves the conversation forward. His partner understands this, and they have real exchanges, not "language lessons." He is well aware when someone responds to him in a teaching fashion, and on those occasions the conversation goes nowhere.

Imagine, for example, a small child playing with a ball. The ball rolls to an adult nearby. The child moves after the ball and the adult leans toward the ball and the approaching child.

Adult: Hi, Sara! Here is your ball.
Child: Me, boolll.
Adult: No, Sara, not *me.* Say, "My. It's *my* ball."
Child: (Trying to reach for ball.) Boolll.
Adult: Not booll, it's aaa, ball, ball. Now you say it.
Child: (Noticing a small bug on the ground.) "Bu, bu, bu." (Delighted with the new discovery, forgets about the ball and the "teaching" adult and begins to play with the bug.

This child was not interested in the lessons the adult was giving her. The adult might have given the child the correct pronunciation, but then let the child's activity continue. As it turned out, the child simply moved on to a more interesting activity and ignored the ball and the adult altogether.

How can caregivers foster the development of language in young children? First of all, begin using language with infants immediately. Talk to them long before they can talk to you. And use real adult talk, not just noises and chatter. Listen to young children and encourage them to listen, too. Make sure that you have a child's attention when you are talking together, and be sure to give him yours. Use labels so that children learn the names of objects and events. And restrain the temptation to rush children or interrupt them. Give them time to say the words they know.

The complex movement from an internal, organized, receptive process to an external, social, expressive process can be readily observed in infants during their first two years. This process of language development has at its foundation the capacity of infants to receive sensory information and their ability to respond and adjust to it. As infants experience their world and coordinate their responses to it, reactions from caregivers are very important. Caregivers encourage the social quality of language when they interact with infants. They also display their individual styles and provide infants with a variety of models. Through this variety of contact infants begin to expand their perception of the world.

Language styles

Adults have learned to adjust their communication patterns for specific situations. From observing adult communication styles, very young children also learn to adapt their words and phrases to the person or the occasion. Probably one of the best examples of a child coordinating language styles is the child who is becoming bilingual. If words help to define our perceptions, does the person who has several words for a particular object or event, because he knows more than one language, experience that object or event differently? We cannot answer that question here. But we can say that very early, children are ready to differentiate their experiences and coordinate experiences with the words appropriate to them.

In the following scene a young child is becoming bilingual. We must assume what he is thinking by what he is doing and saying, but it seems obvious that he has already coordinated quite a lot of experience in two cultures and languages.

A mother is heating tortillas on the stove. Her young son stands nearby talking to her, chattering in baby talk in Spanish. He tells her he is hungry. She smiles and answers him in Spanish, at the same time handing him a warm, soft, rolled-up tortilla. The child takes a bite, relishing it. As he reaches for another bite, he hears the sound of the door opening and someone walking in. He looks up and sees his father entering the kitchen. The father says, "Ummm, something smells good." The child holds out his tortilla and says, "Bite?" Mother hands father his own tortilla. Then she turns back to the stove. Father says, "Thanks anyway, son. I have my own," showing him the tortilla in his hand. Both father and son eat contentedly when a voice from the other room drifts into the kitchen. Father, interrupting his next bite, says to his son, "How about Grandma? Go ask her if she wants a tortilla. . . ." The child runs from the room calling, "Abuelita, Abuelita, quieres tortilla?"

This child, only three years old, is managing to learn two languages, and further, is learning when to use each one. From the beginning, this child had two language

Chapter 8
The
Development of
Knowing and
Language

121

partners—an English-speaking one (his father) and a Spanish-speaking one (his mother). He also had a Spanish-speaking grandmother who lived in his home (who was a partner, too). He started his language learning in the same way as the monolingual child in the earlier part of this chapter. That is, he discovered responses to his cries and vocalizations; he learned to refine his skills at sending messages and to differentiate his sounds; and he learned to sort out the sounds he heard. During this process of learning to tell one sound from another, he discovered that the sounds and rhythms coming to him belonged to two different sets. He came to associate those two sets with particular people (and eventually particular places as well). As he gained words and language structure and began to speak, he learned to tell which sets of words and structures to use when. Meaningful physical prompts and experiences (e.g., seeing his mother cooking) helped him do this. At first he mixed the languages. But by the time he was three years old, he had sorted them out and consistently used each one at the right time and place. Eventually he will even learn to predict which language to speak to a perfect stranger by appearance and setting.

As we implied at the beginning of this section, the skill of using language appropriate to the situation is not limited to children using two languages. All speakers learn early to distinguish between language styles. Listen carefully to the difference between the way two three-year-olds talk to each other and the way they talk to adults. Listen, for example, to the way two children "play house" with each other. The one playing the mother talks the way she perceives adults to talk, while the one playing the baby speaks in a different way altogether. Clearly they have learned that there is one style for talking to peers and another for talking to adults. Children may even distinguish among the adults they speak to. For example, a preschooler may speak differently to her mother at home and to her teacher at school. By listening, you can discover for yourself that children not only use more than one language style but also are aware of the differences.

Let's look back on the major language skills that infants have usually acquired by the end of their second year. They realize that events can be labeled, that they can be repeated, and that they have meaning. They have moved from simple crying sounds, through cooing and babbling, to words—sounds that have agreed-upon meaning. They can share experiences with others, and they can use language to further understand their world. Within two years infants move from simple sensory-motor experiences to abilities that allow them to symbolize events (label objects), be aware of language styles, and combine concepts (linking two and three words). The following exercise is designed to encourage you to see for yourself how language begins to unfold. We hope that actually watching and listening to a young child will make the sequence of developmental abilities we have described more meaningful to you.

Observe an infant or toddler (over a period of several weeks, if possible), watching and listening for the behaviors listed below. Then answer the following questions about each one:
How did the baby behave (quiet, a lot of movement, tense or relaxed)? Describe

the circumstances (at home, in a group setting, in someone else's home)? What do you think the behavior meant (expression of anger, pleasure, hunger, exhaustion)? What do you think the baby hoped to get out of it (bring someone close, be left alone, get attention)?

1. The baby cried:

2. The baby paid attention to a spoken voice:

3. The baby cooed and babbled to himself/herself:

4. The baby expressed eagerness in sounds:

5. The baby expressed displeasure in sounds:

6. The baby expressed satisfaction in sounds:

7. The baby used sounds to indicate recognition:

8. The baby imitated syllables said by someone else:

9. The baby said a word: (When you know that the baby uses the same sound consistently for the same object, you can call the sound a word. It may be a private word—one the baby made up—but it is effectively a word when the sound, tone, behavior, and intention of the baby all convey the same meaning in the same context.)

10. The baby responded to simple commands:

Did you have trouble recording the sounds on paper? You probably found yourself without symbols for some of the sounds you heard. Young infants can make all the sounds of all languages, but they soon begin refining the sounds they make and eventually exclude most of those that do not belong to their culture's language. As adults we are often unable to make some of the sounds we enjoyed as babies. (You may know something about this inability to produce new or forgotten sounds if you have tried to learn a foreign language as an adult.)

Chapter 8
The
Development of
Knowing and
Language

123

Knowing and language interwoven

This chapter has examined the complexity of the interwoven qualities of knowing and language. Both processes begin in simple, undifferentiated ways. By the beginning of the third year, these processes have coordinated themselves to allow infants to achieve abilities in organizing experience, in combining concepts, and in social communication.

As infants explore their world, they seem immediately to blend their internal and external experiences. Knowing that events are repeated and have meaning alllows language to provide labels and store information. Such remembered information provides a larger base from which greater mental combinations of experience can be made. Knowing supports language in its development, and language allows knowing and understanding to expand. As children coordinate these functions, caregivers can assist them in the following ways. Allow them to explore a variety of experiences. Set realistic limits, but encourage reasonable choices and do not squelch activity. If experiences and routines are arranged so that children can make distinctions easily, in other words, if the environment is not confusing, children will more easily see links between experiences. Involve young children in real activities and give them time alone to take in their own information. And finally, take time to observe and appreciate children as they learn. They have sensitive insights to share with us.

Summary thought questions

1. Define "knowing" and "language." What relationship exists between these two processes?

2. What behaviors indicate that a child is developing understanding? Describe at least four of them.

3. Compare your understanding of "sensory-motor knowing" and "intuitive knowing."

4. Describe what is meant by "receptive language." How does it differ from "expressive language" and why is it important?

5. Listen to a child just under three years old. What does language allow this child to do? How is language related to the child's understanding?

Notes

1 John L. Phillips, Jr., *The Origins of Intellect: Piaget's Theory.* (San Francisco, Ca.: W. H. Freeman, 1969), pp. 25-60.

2 Robert Samples, *The Metaphoric Mind* (Menlo Park, Ca.: Addison-Wesley, 1976), p. 103.

Further Reading

Brown, Roger. *A First Language: The Early Years.* Cambridge, Mass.: Harvard University Press, 1973.

Lahane, Stephen. *Help Your Baby Learn: 100 Piaget-Based Activities for the First Two Years of Life.* Englewood Cliffs: Prentice-Hall, 1976.

Ligon, Ernest; Barber, Lucie; and Williams, Herman. *If You Only Knew What Your Baby Was Thinking.* Burlingame, Ca.: Panamedia, Inc., 1973.

Samples, Robert. *The Metaphoric Mind.* Menlo Park, Ca.: Addison-Wesley, 1976.

Lennenberg, H.E. "On Explaining Language." *Science,* 1969, **164**, 635-43.

CHAPTER 9
The Development of Feelings and Self

Feelings, or emotions, give a sense of direction to the individual. This sense of direction is an early indicator of the "self." As caregivers help infants recognize, accept, and value their feelings, learn self-calming devices, and eventually learn to determine when it is appropriate to act on certain feelings, they help infants develop a sense of self. The sense of self is part of what makes each individual unique.

What are emotions?

What are emotions or feelings? Where do they come from? The word emotion comes from a Latin word meaning to move, stir up, agitate, or excite. Emotions come from within the individual, though they may be triggered by an external event. The external event may be real and immediate, or it may be a memory from the past, an anticipation of a future event, or an entirely imaginary event. Whether or not the *event* is, or ever was, real, the *feelings* are real.

Try this exercise to discover that emotions are internal (i.e., that they come from within).

Conjure up a picture of a particularly pleasant or unpleasant experience you have had. Notice the feelings that come with it. Write about those feelings here.

This exercise may or may not have been easy for you. Some people can call forth events better than others.

Do infants also have emotions from calling forth past events, anticipating future ones, and making up imaginary ones? Not at birth. If infants do have emotions at birth, they are related to immediate experiences and sensations. Memory and the ability to anticipate depend on the intellectual development that occurs gradually during the first two years.

That newborn infants do have emotions from the first moments of life is a view on which the gentle birth advocates, such as Dr. Leboyer, the French obstetrician, base their rationale. Until recently it was widely believed that babies did not feel much at birth. If they had sensations, the possibility of emotional response to them was discounted. We know now that infants do have use of their senses at birth, and consequently researchers and caregivers are now questioning the importance of the emotional aspects of what infants feel. Although infants cannot talk about what they experience emotionally at birth, we can see physical reactions. There is evidence that they react to harsh stimulation with tenseness. We once thought that the panicky birth cry and the tightly clenched fists were normal and even necessary. Now that Leboyer and others have demonstrated what happens when you reduce harsh stimuli like bright lights, loud noises, and abrupt changes in temperature, we know that a newborn can be relaxed and peaceful. Some babies born under Leboyer's method even smile right after birth.[1]

In the first weeks of life, infants' emotional responses are not very refined. Very young infants are either in a stirred up state or they are not. They may cry with great intensity, but it is hard to put any labels on what they are feeling. As they mature, however, the stirred-up states begin to become differentiated into familiar adult-like emotions—pleasure, fear, and anger. By the second year you can see most of the finer variations of these basic emotions.

How should caregivers respond to infants' emotions? Let us consider caregivers' responses to the two emotions most caregivers find hardest to deal with, fear and anger. In the next scene we see an infant expressing fear:

We see a baby sitting on the floor playing with a soft rubber ball. She stops playing for a moment, looks around the room, searching. She finds her mother close by, a look of relief passes over her face, then she gives a big smile and continues to play. Then we hear a door open, sounds from the other room, and two people enter. The baby stops playing. One of the people approaches her enthusiastically—holding out her arms, talking warmly and excitedly. The baby stiffens. As the person moves nearer, the baby's whole body attitude is one of moving back, away. She remains in suspended animation until the moment the person's face arrives close to hers. She then lets out an enormous howl. She continues to scream and stiffen even though the person talks soothingly and moves away slightly. She only stops when the person moves away and her mother comes in to soothe and comfort her. She clings to her mother, swallowing her last sobs while keeping a suspicious eye on the stranger.

This child experienced strong feelings, possibly the first of this specific kind in her life. The fears shown here were the result of her attachment to her mother. She had reached a stage where she could tell the difference between her mother and others, and she had developed a fear of the others. Called "stranger anxiety," this is a common and perfectly normal fear. The causes of fear change as infants grow and develop. After the first year or two the fears of noise, strange objects and persons, pain, falling, and sudden movements decrease, while new sources of fear take their place: for instance, imaginary creatures, the dark, animals, and the threat of physical harm. Notice that the movement is away from immediate events and sensations alone to more internal events, imagined, remembered, or predicted. This change is related to the child's growing ability to think and consequently to understand potential dangers.

Dealing with infants' fears

Understanding something about infants' fears is the first step in accepting them. Acceptance is vital if infants are to come to eventually recognize, identify, and

Chapter 9
The
Development of
Feelings
and Self

127

accept their own feelings. Be respectful. Accept all fears as real and valid. Do not minimize the child's feeling, even though the incident that provoked it may seem insignificant to you. Acknowledge the fear, and help the infant to cope with it. Compare the two following responses to a crying, fearful infant:

I know you're afraid right now. I will be here if you need me to help you.

Oh, my poor baby . . . don't be afraid . . . I'll make everything all right . . . I'll never leave you.

By saying, "Don't be afraid," the caregiver in the second example is telling the baby that his feelings are not all right or appropriate. Instead of offering security and helping the infant to find her own ways of coping, the caregiver in the second quote is "saving" the baby, teaching her that she cannot manage on her own. Comforting should be done in a way that leads infants to learn to comfort themselves and to know when to ask for help.

With a little foresight, on the caregiver's part, some fears can be prevented. For example, when caregivers know that a strange situation may frighten infants, they can prepare them gradually. This may be done by introducing aspects of the situation before it happens, telling them what is going to happen, or, when possible, breaking the situation into manageable parts. A familiar person or object may help a baby cope with a new, potentially frightening situation. Giving infants time to adjust is important.

Sometimes it helps if an infant can "relearn" a situation that was once frightening. (This relearning is called conditioning.) For example, a particular object or activity that provokes fear can be proved harmless if it is presented along with something that is pleasant, or if a loved person is present to explain the situation. It may take several introductions. Stop if the infant seems highly anxious and, in a few months, try again.

Don't always look for complicated solutions. Remove the source of fear when that is possible and appropriate. For example, if a child is afraid of the dark, provide a night light.

How do you deal with your own fears? List what you do when you are afraid.

Chapter 9
The
Development of
Feelings
and Self

129

Can you help infants do for themselves what you do for yourself? Did you find that you listed withdrawal and avoidance techniques as well as comfort- and security-seeking? Did you list ways of expressing fears?

The children in the following situations are fearful. Before you respond to the questions after each situation, think about your own coping devices and how you might help a child learn to use appropriate ones.

A nine-month-old child has just been left in the center by his mother, who is late to work. Although she did stay with him a few minutes before handing him over to the caregiver, who happens to be a substitute and new, he started screaming when she hastily said good-bye to him and hurried out the door. He is now sitting on the floor terrified, alternately screaming and sobbing.

Why do you suppose the child is afraid?

What might the caregiver do?

Could this scene have been prevented?

A six-month-old who gets around by scooting backward has managed to get herself caught under a table. She takes a moment to realize she can't scoot out, then panics and begins to cry. Every now and then she tries to raise up and bumps her head, scaring herself even more.

Why is the child afraid?

What might the caregiver do?

Should this scene have been prevented?

Were the children in your solutions given credit for their feelings? Did you have the caregiver acknowledge what the child was obviously feeling? Were the infants rescued, or were they given some help in discovering their own methods for relieving their feelings? Can you see what purpose the fear served in each of these situations? In general, fear serves to protect the individual from danger. In infants, it is fairly easy to see how fear functions, since infants react to falling, to harsh assaults on their senses, and to being separated from the person primarily responsible for their well-being. Fear can protect them from danger. Often a frightened child protects himself by withdrawing, as contrasted to an angry child, who more often lashes out.

Dealing with infants' anger
Anger is the second emotion of infants that may give caregivers difficulty. Look at the following example.

We focus on a peaceful scene in an infant center. Most of the children are outside. Three, however, are playing inside: one, a toddler busy in a corner taking toys off the low open shelves; one, a two-month-old lying on the floor near a caregiver; and one, a toddler who seems to be looking for something to get involved in. The third child notices the baby, and with his stiff-legged gait, strolls over. Dropping down heavily, he reaches suddenly for the baby's

Chapter 9
The
Development of
Feelings
and Self

131

head. The caregiver reaches out and touches the toddler's head softly, saying, "Gently, gently. You may touch, but you have to be gentle." His abrupt motion turns into a light touch, and he strokes for a minute the way he has been stroked. But then he gets more energetic and his stroking becomes a heavy pat. His hand is held back by the caregiver, who once more says, "Gently, gently," as she strokes his head again and holds his hand. But this time his response is different and he lifts his free hand to hit the younger child, an expression of determination crossing his face. He is prevented by the firm grasp of the caregiver. Thwarted in his desires, he turns on her, eyes flashing, and begins to struggle. At the same time he starts to make protesting noises. The scene ends with a very angry little boy being removed from the vicinity of the helpless infant. The last thing we hear is the caregiver's calm voice saying, "I know you're very angry, but I can't let you hurt little Miriam."

Notice that the caregiver dealt respectfully with both infants. She protected the baby, but in doing so made the other child angry. Nevertheless, she treated his anger with respect by accepting (for herself) the fact that he was angry and by acknowledging the fact to him (for his sake). She did not give in to his anger, however, since that would have been inappropriate.

Although it was easy to understand the cause of this toddler's anger, it is not always so easy. It is harder to accept an infant's or a toddler's feelings as real and valid when you do not see any good reason for them. When the cause for anger is not as obvious as it was in this example, adults tend to make remarks like, "Oh, that's nothing to get mad about" or "Oh, come on now, you're not really mad." But feelings are real and respectful caregivers treat them as such. They do not contradict the feelings an infant or toddler expresses, even if their own experience is otherwise. They pay attention and try to reflect what they perceive coming from the child. If an infant or toddler is upset, a caregiver says so. They neither tease nor distract the child by changing the subject. Those approaches say to the child, "What you feel is not important" and discount the importance of recognizing and accepting feelings. One should not have to justify feelings—that they are there is enough.

To accept and reflect feelings, caregivers must manage somehow to be serene, tolerant, and self-controlled. They must be able to be empathetic. But they must not deny their own feelings. Just as was stated in the sixth principle in Chapter 1, caregivers should be honest about how they feel and be able to decide when it is appropriate to express their feelings. Good caregivers also learn how to set aside their own feelings when appropriate, in order to understand what a child is feeling. This is the empathetic relationship. It is important in helping a child recognize, accept, and then cope with his own feelings.

In addition to responding by accepting an infant's feelings and expressing their own when appropriate (which teaches by modeling), caregivers can deal with infants' anger in several other ways. Prevention is sometimes possible. Don't remove all sources of frustration, of course, because that eliminates problem solving, but be sure that infants do not confront too many frustrating problems during their day. For examples, toys should be age appropriate, and toys that do not work should be fixed or removed.

Provide for infants' physical needs. A tired or hungry child is more easily angered than one who is rested and full. Short tempers hinder problem solving, since the child gives up in unproductive anger.

How do you deal with your own anger? List the ways you cope.

Are you satisfied with the ways you cope? Can you teach infants to cope with their anger in some of the same ways? Did you find that you listed a variety of ways in which you express anger, especially anger that you cannot act on directly? A difficulty arises when the built-in responses for emotions are inappropriate and one cannot use the energy that rises with the anger. Then the feelings, and the energy, are blocked. That energy is released through action or expression. You may have mentioned that you express anger through words, physical activity (or even art and music).

A young infant has limited resources for expression. Crying may be all he is capable of. However, crying is a good release valve for infants because it involves both sound and physical activity. The early crying can later become refined physical activity and words as the infant grows in his ability to use his body and language. Caregivers who allow infants to cry in anger also learn to direct an angry toddler's energy to pounding clay, throwing bean bags, and telling people how they feel.

Look at the following situations and assume that the children are feeling angry. Respond to the questions after each brief situation.

A nine-month-old child is playing in his crib with several toys. One toy slips through the crib bars and gets stuck. The harder the infant twists and pulls on the toy, the more stuck it seems to become. He finally begins to cry. An adult appears in the doorway.

Why might the child be angry?

What might an adult do?

What purpose might the anger here serve?

An eight-month-old boy has just discovered a large metal bobby pin. He plays with it for several minutes, gently poking his own fingers and then the carpet. He notices a light socket on the wall nearby and moves toward it with the bobby pin. An adult who has been watching him quickly moves in and removes the bobby pin. The infant startles and then begins to cry.

Why might this child be angry?

What might the caregiver have done?

What purpose might the anger serve?

Could you find a purpose for the anger in each case? If well used, anger mobilizes extra energy for problem solving or gives motivation to keep on trying. Not all problems have satisfactory solutions, of course, and in such a case the anger can only be used as an expression of the frustration felt. This expression can be seen as an aspect of asserting independence (as illustrated by the protests in the second situation).

Could you understand the reasons for the child's anger in each situation? Did that understanding help clarify what the caregiver should do? Did you have the caregiver acknowledge the anger? To what extent did you allow the infants to solve their own problems and calm themselves?

Chapter 9
The
Development of
Feelings
and Self

133

Self-calming techniques

It is important that infants learn ways to calm themselves and not rely solely on others to settle their emotional upsets. Most infants are born with varying degrees of abilities to do this. These abilities are called self-calming devices. At first the techniques are quite simple, just as the infants' emotions are also simple (though intense). The most commonly seen self-calming device is thumb sucking, which may start at birth (or even before). As infants' emotions become more complicated, so do their abilities to deal with them. The variety of self-calming behaviors seen in an infant center setting will give you some idea of how these behaviors work.

Twelve children are engaged in various activities. Two infants are asleep in their cribs in a blocked-off corner of the room. One six-month-old is on the lap of a caregiver, taking her bottle. Two three-month-olds are lying on their backs in a fenced-off corner of the room watching two toddlers who are poking toys through the slats of the fence. All of them are being watched by an adult who also has her eye on a toddler who is headed for the door, apparently intent on some outdoor activity. In another corner of the room, four toddlers are eating a snack, seated at a table with another adult. Suddenly a loud bang from the next room interrupts all activity.

- One infant wakes up and starts to cry, then finds her thumb, turns her head down into the blanket, and goes back to sleep.

- The other sleeping infant startles without waking up, twists around slightly and goes back to sleep.

- The six-month-old taking her bottle stops, looks intensely at the caregiver, gropes with her free hand for something to hang on to, and hangs on tight.

- The two infants on their backs start to cry. One struggles to change his position, gets involved in his effort, and stops crying; the other continues to cry uncomforted.

- The two toddlers that have been watching them stop their activity. One heads for the caregiver who had been watching them. The other heads for his crib, where he knows he will find his special blanket. The child who was on the way outside runs to the caregiver picking up a doll on the way. He stands by the caregiver, stroking the smooth satin dress of the doll.

- Of the children who were having a snack, one cries and cannot comfort himself until the caregiver's voice soothes him saying, "Yes, that was a loud noise and it scared you;" one cries for more food; one cries for Mommy; and one climbs under the table, whimpering.

Some self-calming behaviors are learned, whereas others, like thumb sucking, appear to be innate. A newborn who is tired or frustrated will suck even when no nipple is present. When children are a bit older, thumb or finger sucking still serves in times of stress. Knowing that someone they trust is nearby and checking in with them by glancing toward them or calling to them help children calm themselves.

A baby who is upset or angry is anxious to communicate such information to another individual and to express his feelings about it. This growth of self-calming behavior, from one as simple as sucking to one as complex as sharing important feelings, is a process influenced and supported by social relationships.

What do you do to settle yourself down when you are upset? List your own self-calming devices.

How are these devices similar to or different from those of the infants shown in the infant center scene?

Developing a sense of self

Emotions, and the resultant attempts at self-calming, are among the first signs of the "self" at work. We think of the self as the force that provides the natural thrust toward maturity, guides growth, and gives direction to one's life (both in the long term and from day to day). We believe that the self guides growth toward health and wholeness. By wholeness we mean the integrating of all aspects of development.

Chapter 9
The
Development of
Feelings
and Self

135

Carl Jung described the self as "an inner guiding factor that is different from the conscious personality. . . . It is a regulating center that brings about a constant extension and maturing of the personality."[2]

Abraham Maslow also recognized that the development of a sense of self is vital to growth. His term for that process is "self-actualization." He argued that healthy people are always in the process of self-actualizing. That means they are aware of their potential and, at least at times, they make choices that move them toward it instead of away from it.

What are the characteristics of self-actualizing people? Maslow says that they perceive reality clearly, that they are open to experience, that they tend to be spontaneous and expressive. They have a sense of aliveness. They function well. They are able to be objective and detached. They tend to be creative. They have the ability to love. Above all they have a firm identity, autonomy, uniqueness—a strong sense of self.[3]

Maslow makes it very clear that people come to have these characteristics only when their physical, emotional, and intellectual needs are met. He sets out five levels of needs (see Figure 9.1). Only when the needs of one level are satisfied can a person move on to deal with the needs on the next level.

What are the implications for caregivers in Maslow's levels of needs? Levels 1 and 2 are of primary concern in an infant center. The needs of those levels are usually regulated by licensing requirements. Levels 3, 4, and 5 are more often left up to the staff of the center or the caregiver(s) in a family day care home. This book has taken as its primary focus the top three levels. A look at the principles in Chapter 1 shows little focus on the physical needs of infants, but rather assumes that caregivers will provide for those needs first. They are, after all, the obvious needs. Our aim has been to bring out the needs that must be met after the basic ones have been satisfied. Our aim in Chapter 3 was to show how to serve physical needs in ways that respond to higher needs at the same time.

We mentioned in Chapter 3 and throughout the book that a caregiver should not attempt to meet all the needs of an infant. Maslow also warns of the danger to the sense of self that comes from trying to meet all of an infant's needs all of the time:

> We know already that the main prerequisite of healthy growth is gratification of the basic needs. . . . But we have also learned that unbridled indulgence and gratification has its own dangerous consequences, e.g., psychopathic personality, "orality," irresponsibility, inability to bear stress, spoiling, immaturity, certain character disorders. Research findings are rare but there is now available a large store of clinical and educational experience which allows us to make a reasonable guess that the young child needs not only gratification; he needs also to learn the limitations that the physical world puts upon his gratifications. . . . This means control, delay, limits, renunciation, frustration-tolerance, and discipline. Only to the self-disciplined and responsible person can we say, "Do as you will, and it will probably be all right."[4]

All creatures have a need for stress, for problems. A lack of problems creates deficiencies. *Optimum* (not maximum or minimum) stress gives children an opportunity to try out their own powers, to develop their strength and will by

Chapter 9
The
Development of
Feelings
and Self

137

Figure 9.1
Maslow's hierarchy of physical,
emotional, and intellectual needs

LEVEL 5
Self-Actualization

(Needs that relate to
achievement and self
expression, to realize ones
potential)

LEVEL 4
Esteem   Self Esteem

(Needs that relate to maintaining satisfying
relationships with others—to be valued,
accepted, and appreciated. To have status)

LEVEL 3
Love   Belonging   Closeness

(Needs that relate to love, affection, care, attention, and
emotional support by another)

LEVEL 2
Safety   Security   Protection

(Needs that relate to physical safety to avoid external dangers or
anything that might harm the individual)

LEVEL 1
Sex   Activity   Exploration   Manipulation   Novelty
Food   Air   Water   Temperature   Elimination   Rest   Pain/violence

(Needs that are essential body needs—to have access to food, water, air, sexual
gratification, warmth, etc.)

Source:
Abraham H. Maslow, Motivation and Personality (New York: Harper & Row, 1970), p. 72.

pushing against something. Problems, obstacles, even pain and grief, can be looked upon as beneficial for development of a sense of self.

Compare a soft life without problems to a soft toy. The infant explores a soft toy, cuddles it, appreciates its yielding qualities. But we have noticed that eventually infants seek out hard toys and objects. Hard objects do not yield and change shape. Because they stand firm and resist the touch, they are easier to get to know and understand. Infants evidently recognize the benefits of this firmness, because they seek it out. Is it possible that children also seek out challenges when life is too soft and easy? Do they make problems when none is immediately available? Do they create problems in order to have something to push against? In Chapter 4 we discussed problem solving as promoting physical, intellectual, and emotional development. Here we are talking about problem solving as a means of promoting a sense of self.

What can caregivers do to help a child develop a sense of self? We have already mentioned responding to needs appropriately and promoting problem solving. In addition, we want to make four other specific suggestions that draw on some of the abilities of infants we have discussed.

Help children learn to pay attention to what their perceptions, feelings, and bodies tell them. As we stated in the first part of this chapter, don't contradict their perceptions with statements like, "That soup is not hot!" or "That didn't hurt, now did it?" Don't interrupt when they are obviously deeply involved in something. When you break in you are asking them to pay attention to *you*. Infants have the ability to get the most out of whatever it is they experience, so let them fully experience it. And be sure to allow periods without stimulation. Let children have peace and quiet so that they can hear their inner music, feel their inner urges, and see their inner images.

Don't push development. Provide a prepared environment and good relationships, and then trust that children's sense of self serves as an inner director and that they will do what they need to do when it comes to conquering developmental tasks like crawling, walking, or talking. When they have very thoroughly done what they need to do at one stage, they will become bored and will move on. When pushed, a child feels conflict with his developing sense of self.

Give choices. Maslow says this:

In the normal development of the healthy child, it is now believed that, much of the time, if he is given a really free choice, he will choose what is good for his growth. This he does because it tastes good, feels good, gives pleasure or *delight*. This implies that *he* "knows" better than anyone else what is good for him.[5]

Encourage children to develop independence and become self-sufficient. Growing means letting go. One only learns to walk when one is willing to let go, to take risks. Caregivers can help children let go by allowing them to take reasonable risks and by providing warmth, confidence, reasonable safety, and a home base. The choice of when to let go is up to the child.

To summarize the suggestions:

- Respond to needs appropriately.
- Promote problem solving.
- Help children learn to pay attention.
- Don't push development.
- Give choices.
- Encourage children to develop independence and become self-sufficient.

You may notice that these suggestions are related to and in some cases restatements of the principles of caregiving listed in Chapter 1. All of them involve respecting the infant, which is what the principles are based on. The infant's sense of self is nourished by the respectful infant-adult relationship that these principles promote.

What about your own sense of self? Try this exercise. Think about how you determine what your needs are, how you move from something safe and familiar to something new and unknown, how you arrange to have quiet, unstimulating periods to be alone with yourself, how you strive to fulfill your potential. Summarize your thoughts here.

**Chapter 9
The
Development of
Feelings
and Self**

139

Are you aware of your own feelings, your own needs? Do you know how to pay attention to what goes on inside you and make decisions about when to act on inner messages? Do you promote your own growth? What better model for a child than an adult with a well-developed sense of self.

Getting in touch with your own sense of self was in part the reason for our workbook approach. Go back to Chapter 1 and review some of your values, attitudes, and goals, and see if your thinking or perceptions have changed since reading and working your way through this book.

What kinds of changes have taken place?

Sometimes caregivers who work in institutions, especially large ones, are not respected as individuals and in turn have trouble relating to the infants they care for as individuals. We hope this book has helped you not only to value yourself and demand respect from others but also to find ways to treat each infant in your care with an appreciation for his uniqueness. The following poem by Kahlil Gibran speaks of the unfolding of self-knowledge:[6]

> Your hearts know in silence the secrets
> of the days and the nights.
> But your ears thirst for the sound of
> your heart's knowledge.
> You would know in words that which
> you have always known in thought,
> You would touch with your fingers the
> naked body of your dreams.
>
> And it is well you should.
> The hidden well-spring of your soul must
> needs rise and run murmuring to the sea;
> And the treasure of your infinite depths
> would be revealed to your eyes.
> But let there be no scales to weigh your
> unknown treasure;
> And seek not the depths of your knowledge
> with staff or sounding line.
> For self is a sea boundless and measure-
> less.
>
> Say not, "I have found the truth," but
> rather, "I have found a truth."
> Say not, "I have found the path of the soul,"
> say rather, "I have met the soul walking upon my path."
> For the soul walks upon all paths.
> The soul walks not upon a line, neither
> does it grow like a reed.
> The soul unfolds itself, like a lotus
> of countless petals.

Summary thought questions

Chapter 9
The
Development of
Feelings
and Self

141

1. Think of examples of fear and anger in a very young child. Why is it important for the caregiver to be able to distinguish between these two feelings?

2. How can caregivers help infants handle frustrations and encourage self-calming behavior?

3. How can the information on caregiving in Chapter 3 be used to develop a sense of self in infants?

4. How can caregivers respond to infants in ways that promote individuality in a center setting?

Notes

1 Frederick Leboyer, *Birth Without Violence* (New York: Random House, 1978).

2 M. L. von Franz, "The Process of Individuation," in C. G. Jung and others, *Man and His Symbols* (New York: Doubleday, 1964), p. 162.

3 Abraham H. Maslow, *Toward a Psychology of Being,* 2d ed. (New York: D. van Nostrand Company, 1968), p. 157. © 1968 by Litton Educational Publishing, Inc.

4 Maslow, pp. 163-64.

5 Maslow, p. 198.

6 Reprinted from *The Prophet*, by Kahlil Gibran, with permission of the publisher, Alfred A. Knopf, Inc. Copyright 1923 by Kahlil Gibran; renewed copyright 1951 by Administrators C.T.A. of Kahlil Gibran Estate, and Mary G. Gibran.

Further reading

Assagioli, Roberto. *The Act of Will*. Baltimore: Penguin Books, 1973.

Brazelton, T. Berry. *Infants and Mothers*. New York: Delta Books, 1969.

Hendricks, Gay, and Wills, Russell. *The Centering Book*. Englewood Cliffs: Prentice-Hall, 1975.

Lee, Dorothy. *Valuing the Self*. Englewood Cliffs: Prentice-Hall, 1976.

Lynn, D. B. *The Father: His Role in Development*. Monterey, Ca.: Brooks/Cole, 1974.

Maslow, A. H. *Toward a Psychology of Being*. 2d ed. New York: D. van Nostrand Company, 1968.

Samuels, Mike and Nancy. *Seeing with the Mind's Eye*. New York: Random House, 1975.

This chart shows how to set up both the physical and the social environment to promote development. Rather than emphasize the age of the child, we have emphasized the developmental sequence, since rates of development vary a great deal among normal children.

LEVEL I: The beginning of life.

Area of development	Physical environment	Social environment
PHYSICAL	APPROPRIATE TOYS AND EQUIPMENT	ADULT ROLE

Large muscles

- infant's primary task is head control
- lifts head briefly
- can turn head to clear nose for breathing
- most arm and leg movements are reflexive and are not under infant's conscious control

Small muscles

- cannot control hands—often keeps them clenched
- grasps whatever is put into hands because of reflexive action
- stares at objects, especially faces; begins to coordinate eyes

- crib or bassinet, a place to feel secure while sleeping
- mat, rug, or blanket in a safe space to lie unencumbered; room to move around
- few toys needed yet as environment is stimulating enough
- faces are interesting, and so is a bright-colored scarf
- don't put rattles or toys into his hands, since he can't let go of them

- use sensitive observation to determine infant's needs
- provide a feeling of security when necessary (wrap the infant in a blanket and put him in a small enclosed space)
- let infant experience wide open space like the floor at times
- provide peace and quiet and a minimal amount of stimulation—he'll get enough with the people he associates with (caregiver and other children)
- put him in a safe spot where he can be part of the center but not overstimulated

143

LEVEL I (Cont.)

Area of development

EMOTIONAL/SOCIAL

Feelings and self-awareness

- infant shows only satisfaction or dissatisfaction
- infant does not differentiate self from the rest of the world

Social

- may smile
- make eye contact
- is soothed by faces
- responds to being held

INTELLECTUAL

- can coordinate eyes and follow objects or faces as they move
- responds to faces or objects he sees
- sucks and gums objects that come near his mouth
- displays reflexes that are the beginnings of the sensory skills which in turn provide the basis for the development of intellectual skills

LANGUAGE

- listens
- cries
- responds to voices

Physical environment

APPROPRIATE TOYS AND EQUIPMENT

- infant needs to be where he is safe and secure and his needs can be easily met
- large pen provides safety from more mobile toddlers (should be large enough to hold both adults and children)

- infant needs an interesting yet safe environment with a limited variety of soft, washable, colorful toys to be looked at or sucked on (be sure there are no small parts to come off and be swallowed)
- allow space for infant to move freely (though he can't yet go anywhere)
- don't prop in infant seat or other restrictive device

- at this level people are more important for language development than is physical environment
- set up environment so that infant's needs are easily met and he doesn't have to wait for long periods of time

Social environment

ADULT ROLE

- call infant by name
- encourage infant to focus on caregiving tasks
- respond to infant's messages and try to determine real needs (remember that dissatisfaction is not always due to hunger)
- provide for attachment needs by having a consistent caregiver
- hold during feeding
- give infant opportunity to be in contact with other infants

- minimum adult interference: infant should be free to develop at his own rate
- give him faces to look at (especially that of his primary caregiver) and opportunities to see, touch, and gum objects
- don't force anything on him
- put him on his back occasionally

- listen to the infant
- try to interpret his cries
- talk to infant, especially during caregiving times; tell him what will happen; give time for a response; tell him what is happening as it happens

LEVEL II: The stage of development of many normal infants around the third month of life.

Area of development

PHYSICAL

Large muscles

- beginning to lose reflexes and have voluntary control of arms and legs
- can lift head and control it better when held in upright position

Small muscles

- grasp reflex no longer takes over hands all the time
- reaches for objects with both arms but with hands fisted
- swipes and misses

EMOTIONAL/SOCIAL

Feelings and self-awareness

- shows wider variety of feelings and uses voice to express them
- begins to see hands and feet belong to him and begins to explore them, as well as face, eyes, and mouth, with hands
- begins to recognize primary caregiver
- responds differently to different people
- coos and babbles when talked to

INTELLECTUAL

- responds to what he sees
- attends longer than at first
- looks from one object to another
- can hold object on his own and manipulate to some extent
- gives signs of remembering
- when he hears a noise, he looks for the source
- looks and sucks at the same time, but has to stop sucking to listen

Physical environment

APPROPRIATE TOYS AND EQUIPMENT

- large playpen—big enough for care-givers and several infants
- variety of washable objects within reach of infant for him to look at and stretch for
- rug or mat for infant to lie on (no infant seats or other restric-tive devices)

- mirrors are responded to and begin to give the child a self-image

- some interesting toys and objects for the infant at this level of development are:
  bright scarves
  soft balls
  rattles
  squeeze toys
  plastic keys
  large plastic beads

Social environment

ADULT ROLE

- sit with child periodically and watch attentively
- respond when called for
- don't continually distract with unnecessary noise or talk: entertainment isn't necessary
- allow infant freedom to explore through looking, sucking, stretching, and reaching

- provide for attachment needs as infant needs to develop a primary relationship
- recognize and respect feelings of infant: talk about what infant seems to be expressing, especially during caregiving

- encourage exploration and curiosity by providing a variety of small objects of different textures, shapes, and sizes
- allow child freedom and peace to explore by putting him on his back in a safe area large enough for him to move freely
- provide for interaction with other infants

145

LEVEL II (Cont.)

Area of development	Physical environment	Social environment
LANGUAGE	*APPROPRIATE TOYS AND EQUIPMENT*	*ADULT ROLE*
• listens attentively • coos, whimpers, gurgles, and makes a variety of other sounds • cries less often • "talks" to self as well as to others, particularly primary caregiver	• people are still more important than equipment or objects for language development • some toys do give auditory experiences—let him try making noise with bells, rattles, and squeaky toys	• talk to infant, especially during caregiving routines—prepare him ahead of time for what is going to happen • respond to babbling and cooing; play sound games with the infant

---

LEVEL III: The stage of development of many normal infants around the sixth month of life.

Area of development	Physical environment	Social environment
PHYSICAL	*APPROPRIATE TOYS AND EQUIPMENT*	*ADULT ROLE*
Large muscles • has control of head • turns from back to stomach and stomach to back • may move from place to place by rolling • may creep or inch forward or backward • may almost get to sitting position while rolling over	• needs more open space and freedom than before • needs a variety of textures under his body—hard floor, rugs, grass, wooden deck, etc. • needs interesting objects to move and reach toward • place objects far enough from him so that he has to work to get them	• provide plenty of room and motivation for moving around as well as manipulating and grasping objects • provide for interaction with other infants • don't put infant into positions he can't get into by himself
Small muscles • reaches with one arm and can grasp at will • holds objects and manipulates them • can grasp with thumb and forefinger but not well yet • changes objects from one hand to the other		

146

Area of development	**Physical environment**	**Social environment**
EMOTIONAL/SOCIAL	*APPROPRIATE TOYS AND EQUIPMENT*	*ADULT ROLE*

EMOTIONAL/SOCIAL

Feelings and self-awareness

- displays a wider variety of feelings
- smiles at self in mirror
- is becoming aware of body parts
- sees difference between self and rest of the world
- responds to name
- has taste preferences
- may want to start self-feeding

Physical environment:

- safe space large enough for exploration and social interactions will promote relationships

Social environment:

- talk to infant, especially during caregiving; place special emphasis on naming body parts
- call child by name
- encourage child to take over self-help skills as he is able

Social

- may respond with fear to strangers
- calls to primary caregiver for help
- enjoys games with people like peek-a-boo

Social environment:

- provide for attachment needs and let child use primary caregiver to provide security in presence of strangers
- play games like peek-a-boo

INTELLECTUAL

- is visually alert a good part of waking hours
- recognizes familiar objects
- can see and reach for an object he wants
- can pick up and manipulate objects
- looks for dropped objects
- can use several senses at once
- memory is developing

Physical environment:

- infant continues to enjoy all the toys and objects listed in Level II under Intellectual Development
- can now appreciate a wider variety of objects at once
- place objects around a safe area so that he has reason to move around and reach for them

Social environment:

- allow child freedom to explore
- change or rearrange objects in the environment periodically
- provide for interaction with other infants

LANGUAGE

- responds to different voice tones and inflections
- has more control of sounds produced
- uses a variety of sounds to express feelings
- imitates tones and inflections

Physical environment:

- cloth or cardboard books

Social environment:

- respond to child's communication
- talk to child especially during caregiving routines
- during play times, comment on what the child is doing if appropriate (be careful not to interrupt so the words get in the way of the experience)

LEVEL IV: The stage of development of many normal infants around the ninth month of life.

Area of development	Physical environment	Social environment
PHYSICAL	*APPROPRIATE TOYS AND EQUIPMENT*	*ADULT ROLE*

Area of development

PHYSICAL

Large muscles

- crawls
- may crawl stiff legged
- may crawl while holding object in hand
- pulls to stand on furniture
- may stand alone
- may or may not be able to get back down from standing
- gets into sitting position
- may move along holding onto furniture

Small muscles

- can pick up small objects easily with thumb and forefinger
- explores and manipulates with forefinger
- growing in eye-hand coordination

EMOTIONAL/SOCIAL

Feelings and self-awareness

- recognizes self in mirror
- clearly attached to primary care-giver and may fear separation from him or her
- rejects things he doesn't want

Social

- feeds self biscuit
- drinks from cup holding handle
- is usually a willing performer if asked
- is becoming sensitive to and interested in the moods and activities of others
- teases
- anticipates events

Physical environment

APPROPRIATE TOYS AND EQUIPMENT

- infant needs more room to explore—a greater variety of objects, textures, experiences, toys
- plastic or wooden cars and trucks, play or real telephones, blocks, dolls, balls of different sizes, nesting toys
- pillows and low platforms (or steps) can be added to the environment to provide a variety of levels for the child to explore
- rails or low furniture needed for standing or cruising

- needs the tools for self-help skills such as cup and spoon

Social environment

ADULT ROLE

- watch for child who stands up but can't sit back down; help when he indicates he is stuck
- be sensible about helping the child who gets stuck: don't rescue; but promote problem solving
- provide open space and safe climbing opportunities
- allow child to explore with little adult interference
- encourage infant to use manipulative skills, such as pulling off socks, opening doors, taking apart nesting toys, etc.

- provide enough of a schedule for infant to come to anticipate the sequence of events
- allow opportunities for uninterrupted concentration
- encourage problem solving
- don't help until he's really stuck
- allow him to discover the consequences of his behavior whenever it is safe to do so

LEVEL IV (Cont.)

Area of development	Physical environment	Social environment
INTELLECTUAL	*APPROPRIATE TOYS AND EQUIPMENT*	*ADULT ROLE*
• remembers games and toys from previous days • anticipates return of people • can concentrate and not get interrupted • pulls cover off toy he has seen hidden • enjoys taking things out of container and putting them back • solves simple manipulative problems • interested in discovering the consequences of his behavior	• the objects and toys listed under physical development are also appropriate for promoting intellectual development • also provide interesting and safe objects from the adult world: pots, pans, wooden spoons, and junk such as discarded boxes, both big and little (infants appreciate real objects as much as toys)	• provide the opportunity for infant to become self-assertive • help child to interpret the effect of his actions on others • give plenty of opportunities for child to develop self-help skills • help child express separation fears, accept them, and help him deal with them • provide for attachment to primary caregiver • provide good models for child (adults who express honest feelings, neither minimized nor exaggerated)
LANGUAGE		
• pays attention to conversations • may respond to words other than own name • may carry out simple commands • uses words such as "mama" and "dada" • has intonation • may repeat a sequence of sounds • yells	• appreciates a greater variety of picture books	• include infant in conversation • don't talk about him if he's present until you include him (especially important at this stage) • promote interactions with other infants • respond to infant's sounds • encourage use of words • ask questions the infant can respond to

---

LEVEL V: The stage of development of many normal infants around the first year of life.

Area of development	Physical environment	Social environment
PHYSICAL	*APPROPRIATE TOYS AND EQUIPMENT*	*ADULT ROLE*
Large muscles • can stand without holding on • may walk but probably prefers to crawl • climbs up and down stairs • may climb out of crib	• needs lots of space both indoors and outdoors to enjoy crawling and practice walking • needs lots of objects to manipulate, explore, and experiment with	• provide for safety and plenty of movement • don't push child to walk; allow him to decide when he is finished with crawling

LEVEL V (Cont.)

Area of development	Physical environment	Social environment
PHYSICAL	APPROPRIATE TOYS AND EQUIPMENT	ADULT ROLE

Small muscles
- may use both hands at the same time for different things
- uses thumb well
- shows preference for one hand
- may undress self or untie shoes

- the beginning walker will soon enjoy push-and-pull toys

EMOTIONAL/SOCIAL

Feelings and self-awareness
- shows wide variety of emotions and responds to those of others
- fears strangers and new places
- shows affection
- shows moods and preferences
- may know difference between his possessions and others'

- objects are less important than people

- provide for self-help skills
- acknowledge his possessions and help protect them
- give approval
- set reasonable limits
- accept uncooperative behavior as sign of self-assertion
- give choices
- return affection
- accept and help him deal with fears and frustrations

Social
- feeds self
- helps dress self
- obeys commands
- seeks approval but is not always cooperative

INTELLECTUAL
- is good at finding hidden objects
- memory is increased
- solves problems
- uses trial and error method effectively
- explores new approaches to problems
- thinks about actions before doing them (sometimes)
- imitates people who are not present

- children at this level enjoy most of the toys and household objects already mentioned but use them in more sophisticated ways
- also enjoy large beads to string, large Lego blocks, small building blocks, stacking cones, wooden snap trains, etc.

- promote active problem solving
- provide for interaction with other children
- set up environment so that child sees new and more complex ways to use toys and equipment

LEVEL V (Cont.)

Area of development

LANGUAGE

- knows words stand for objects
- begins to sound like he speaks the language of his parents (uses same sounds and intonations)
- uses gestures to express self
- may say two to eight words

Physical environment

APPROPRIATE TOYS AND EQUIPMENT

- toy telephones, dolls, and books promote language development at this level
- any toy can become a reason to talk as the child plays
- music promotes language development

Social environment

ADULT ROLE

- promote interaction among children; children learn to talk from adults, but they practice as they play with other children
- give simple instructions
- play games with child
- sing songs and do finger plays
- encourage expression of feelings
- fill in missing words and expand utterances for child when responding

---

LEVEL VI: The stage of development of many normal children around the eighteenth month of life.

Area of development

PHYSICAL

Large muscles

- walks fast and well
- falls seldom
- runs awkwardly
- walks up stairs holding a hand

Small muscles

- can use crayon to scribble as well as imitate marks

Physical environment

APPROPRIATE TOYS AND EQUIPMENT

- needs room to walk and run
- enjoys taking walks if adult isn't too goal oriented
- enjoys plenty of sensory experiences such as water play and scribbling

Social environment

ADULT ROLE

- keep the environment full and interesting; may need to change arrangement periodically and introduce new toys
- promote interactions among children
- allow for enough physical exercise

EMOTIONAL/SOCIAL

- imitates adults in dramatic play
- interested in helping with chores
- interested in dressing process; can undress to some extent
- may be beginning to get some bladder and bowel control

- provide the tools for dramatic play such as dress-up clothes, dolls, housekeeping equipment, dishes, etc.

- allow child to help as he is able
- set limits and gently but firmly enforce them
- enourage self-help skills
- help children with their inter- actions and help them talk through aggressive situations

LEVEL VI (Cont.)

Area of development

INTELLECTUAL

- can begin to solve problems in his head
- rapid increase of language development
- beginning of ability to fantasize and role play

LANGUAGE

- may use words to gain attention
- can indicate wants with some words and lots of gestures
- may know ten or more words
- enjoys picture books

Physical environment

APPROPRIATE TOYS AND EQUIPMENT

- provide a variety of toys available on low shelves for child to choose
- a child of this level enjoys small people and animals, doll houses, containers filled with small objects, measuring cups and spoons, etc.
- books with clear and simple pictures

Social environment

ADULT ROLE

- provide a number of choices for each child
- help child to work on a problem uninterrupted
- encourage use of language

- provide a variety of experiences and help child put language to them
- ask questions and encourage child to ask them too
- read aloud

LEVEL VII: The stage of development of many normal children around the second year of life.

Area of development

PHYSICAL

Large muscles

- runs well
- walks up and down stairs
- kicks and throws a ball

Small muscles

- holds spoon, fork, and cup well but may spill
- can use a paint brush

Physical environment

APPROPRIATE TOYS AND EQUIPMENT

- child of this level can begin to use some of the equipment found in nursery schools, including crayons, paints, manipulative table toys, clay, and play dough
- field trips and excursions on simple level help expand the two-year-old's world beyond the center

Social environment

ADULT ROLE

- allow for plenty of physical and sensory experiences
- encourage child to find new ways to combine and use familiar toys and equipment
- offer choices

LEVEL VI (Cont.)

Area of development

EMOTIONAL/SOCIAL

- understands personal property concepts ("That's mine—that's Daddy's.")
- tends to hoard possessions—doesn't share
- asserts independence ("me do it!")
- takes pride in accomplishments
- can completely undress and partially dress self
- may say "no" even to things he wants

INTELLECTUAL

- language development is dramatic
- memorizes phrases of songs
- can identify pictures of common objects
- can obey two simple commands without visual clues (if he wants to)
- can work simple puzzles

LANGUAGE

- uses personal pronouns (I, me, you) but not always correctly
- refers to self by name
- uses two- and three-word sentences
- may know as many as 50 to 200 words
- talks about what he is doing

Physical environment

APPROPRIATE TOYS AND EQUIPMENT

- provide space for personal possessions (cubbies or boxes)

- provide books, puzzles, records in addition to toys listed under Physical Development

- provide a good variety of books (child can use them carefully)
- pictures at child's eye level around the room, changed often, gives child something to talk about

Social environment

ADULT ROLE

- respect child's need to hold on to his possessions
- model sharing rather than require it
- allow child to try things by himself, even when you know you can do it better or faster
- help him have accomplishments he can take pride in

- provide a variety of choices of materials to use and ways to spend time
- give freedom to use materials in creative ways
- allow exploration

- encourage conversation both between children and between child and adult
- help child to speculate ("I wonder what would happen if . . .")
- go places and talk about what you do and see
- encourage verbalization of feelings and wants
- help children begin to talk out differences instead of solely relying on hitting, kicking, and other negative physical behaviors

REFERENCES

CHAPTER 2

Gerber, M. "Respecting Infants: The Loczy Model of Infant Care," *Supporting the Growth of Infants, Toddlers, and Parents.* in E. Jones, ed., Pasadena, Ca.: Pacific Oaks College, 1979, pp. 37-45.

Pikler, E. "Learning of Motor Skills on the Basis of Self-Induced Movements." *Exceptional Infant Studies in Abnormalities,* Vol. 2. New York: Brunner/Mazel, 1971.

Pikler, E. "Some Contributions to the Study of the Gross Motor Development of Children." *Journal of Genetic Psychology.* 1968, **3**, 27-39.

Pikler, E. "Data on Gross Motor Development of the Infant." *Early Child Development and Care.* 1972, **1**, 297-310.

Pikler, E., and Tardos, A. "Some Contributions to the Study of Infants' Gross Motor Activities." XVI International Congress of Applied Psychology. Amsterdam: Swets and Zeitlinger, 1969.

CHAPTER 3

Gerber, M. "Respecting Infants: The Loczy Model of Infant Care," in E. Jones, ed., *Supporting the Growth of Infants, Toddlers, and Parents.* Pasadena, Ca.: Pacific Oaks College, 1979.

CHAPTER 4

Assagioli, R. *The Act of Will.* Baltimore: Penguin Books, 1973.

Brazelton, T. B., with Main, M. "Are There Too Many Sights and Sounds in Your Baby's World?" *Redbook,* September 1971.

Bromwich, R. M. "Stimulation in the First Year of Life? A Perspective on Infant Development." *Young Children,* January 1977.

Bruner, J. S. *The Relevance of Education.* New York: W. W. Norton, 1971.

Canfield, J., and Wells, H. *100 Ways to Enhance Self-Concept in the Classroom.* Englewood Cliffs: Prentice-Hall, 1976.

Gerber, M. "Respecting Infants: The Loczy Model of Infant Care" in E. Jones, ed., *Supporting the Growth of Infants, Toddlers, and Parents.* Pasadena, Ca.: Pacific Oaks College, 1979.

Maslow, A. H. *Toward a Psychology of Being,* 2d ed. New York: D. van Nostrand Company, 1968.

CHAPTER 5

Bromwich, R. M. "Stimulation in the First Year of Life? A Perspective on Infant Development." *Young Children,* January 1977.

Gerber, M. "Respecting Infants: The Loczy Model of Infant Care," in E. Jones, ed., *Supporting the Growth of Infants, Toddlers, and Parents,* Pasadena, Ca.: Pacific Oaks College, 1979.

Gordon, I. J. *On Early Learning: The Modifiability of Human Potential.* Washington D.C.: Association for Supervision and Curriculum Development, NEA, 1971.

Hunt, J. McV. *Intelligence and Experience.* New York: The Ronald Press, 1961.

Ferguson, J. "Creating Growth-Producing Environments for Infants and Toddlers," in E. Jones, ed., *Supporting the Growth of Infants, Toddlers, and Parents.* Pasadena, Ca.: Pacific Oaks College, 1979.

Jones, E. "Excess and Ecstasy in the Lives of Children." Unpublished paper, Pacific Oaks College, n.d.

Lambie, D., Bond, J., and Weikart, D. *Home Teaching with Mothers and Infants.* Ypsilanti: High/Scope Educational Research Foundation, 1974.

Maslow, A. H. *Toward a Psychology of Being,* 2d ed. New York: D. van Nostrand Company, 1968.

Norman, M. "Substitutes for Mother." *Human Behavior,* February 1978.

Ruopp, R., et al. *Final Report of the National Day Care Study. Children at the Center: Summary Findings and Their Implications.* Cambridge, Mass: ABT Associates, 1979.

CHAPTER 6

Ainsworth, M. D. "Mother-Infant Interaction in the Feeding Situation," in A. Ambrose, ed., *Stimulation in Early Infancy.* London: Academic Press, 1969.

Bradly, R. H., and Caldwell, B. M. "The Relation of Infants' Home Environments to Mental Test Performance at Fifty-Four Months: A Follow-up Study." *Child Development,* 1976, **47**, 1172-74.

Brazelton, T. B., Koslowski, B. and Main, M. "The Origins of Reciprocity: The Early Mother-Infant Interaction," in M. Lewis and L. Rosenblum, eds., *The Effect of the Infant on Its Caregiver.* New York: John Wiley & Sons, 1973.

Bowlby, J. *Attachment and Loss, Vol I: Attachment.* London: Hogarth, 1969.

Caldwell, B. M., Wright, C., Honig, A. S., and Tannenbaum, J. "Infant Day Care and Attachment." *American Journal of Orthopsychiatry,* 1970, **40**, No. 37.

Elardo, P. T., and Caldwell, B. M. "The Kramer Adventure: A School for the Future?" *Childhood Education,* January, 1974.

Fowler, W., and Khan, N. "A Follow-up Investigation of Later Development of Infants in Enriched Group Care." Urbana, Ill.: ERIC, 1976. (Document No. ED 093 506.)

Harlow, H. "The Nature of Love," *American Psychology,* 1958, **13**.

Harlow, H. "Social Deprivation in Monkeys." *Scientific American,* 1962, **207**.

Kagan, J., Kearsley, R. B., and Zelazo, P. "The Effects of Infant Day Care on Psychological Development." ERIC Newsletter, 1976, **10**, No. 2.

Klaus, H., and Kennel, J. *Maternal-Infant Bonding.* St. Louis, Mo.: Mosby, 1976.

Lozoff, B., Brittenham, G., Trause, M. A., Kennel, J., and Klaus, H. "The Mother-Newborn Relationship: Limits of Adaptability." *Journal of Pediatrics,* July 1977.

Murphy, L. "Later Outcomes of Early Infant and Mother Relationships," in L. J. Sonte et al., eds., *Competent Infant.* New York: Basic Books, 1973.

Parke, R. O., and O'Leary, S. "Father-Mother-Infant Interaction in the Newborn Period: Some Findings, Some Observations, Some Unresolved Issues," in K. Riegel and J. Meacham, eds., *The Developing Individual in a Changing World. Vol. 2. Social and Environmental Issues.* The Hague: Mouton, 1975.

Piaget, J. *The Construction of Reality in the Child.* New York: Basic Books, 1937.

Skeels, H. M. "Adult Status of Children with Contrasting Early Life Experience." *Monographs of the Society of Research in Child Development,* 1966, **31**.

Spitz, R. A. "Hospitalization: An Inquiry into the Genesis of Psychiatric Conditions in Early Childhood," in A. Freud, et al., eds., *The Psychoanalytic Study of the Child.* New York: International University Press, 1945.

Yarrow, L. J. "The Development of Focused Relationships During Infancy," in B. Staub, and J. Hellmuth, eds., *Exceptional Infant,* Vol I. Seattle: Special Child Publications, 1967.

CHAPTER 7

Ambron, S. *Child Development.* New York: Holt, Rinehart and Winston, 1975.

Baley Scales of Infant Development. New York: The Psychological Corp., 1969.

Bower, T.G.R. *Development in Infancy.* San Francisco: W. H. Freeman, 1974.

Haaf, R. A., and Bell, R. Q. "Facial Dimension in Visual Discrimination by Human Infants." *Child Development,* 1976, **38**, 895.

Haynes, U. *A Developmental Approach to Casefinding.* U.S. Department of Health, Education, and Welfare: Public Health Service Publication No. 2017, 1967.

Levine, S. "Stimulation in Infancy." *Scientific American* Reprint No. 436, San Francisco: W. H. Freeman, May 1960.

Mussen, P. H., Conger, J. J., and Kagan, J. *Child Development and Personality,* 4th ed. New York: Harper & Row, 1974.

Pikler, E. "Learning of Motor Skills on the Basis of Self-Induced Movements." *Exceptional Infant Studies in Abnormalities.* Vol 2. New York: Brunner/Mazel, 1971.

Pikler, E. "Some Contributions to the Study of the Gross Motor Development of Children." *Journal of Genetic Psychology,* 1968, **3**, 27-39.

Samples, R. *The Metamorphic Mind.* Menlo Park, Ca.: Addison-Wesley, 1976.

CHAPTER 8

Ainsworth, M. D., and Wittig, B. A. "Attachment and Exploratory Behavior of One-Year-Olds in a Strange Situation," in B. M. Foss, ed., *Determinants of Infant Behavior,* Vol. 4. New York: John Wiley & Sons, 1972.

Aldrich, C. A., Norval, M. A., Knop, C., and Venegas, F. "The Crying of Newly Born Babies, IV: Follow-up Study after Additional Nursing Care Had Been Given." *Journal of Pediatrics,* 1946. **27**.

Ambron, S. *Child Development.* New York: Holt, Rinehart and Winston, 1975.

Beckwith, L. "Relationships Between Attributes of Mothers and Their Infants' IQ Scores." *Child Development,* 1971, **42**, No. 4.

Bower, T.G.R. *Development in Infancy.* San Francisco: W. H. Freeman, 1974.

Brown, R., and Bellugi, U. "Three Processes in the Child's Acquisition of Syntax." *Harvard Educational Review,* 1964, **34**.

Carew, J. V., Chan, I., and Halfar, C. *Observing Intelligence in Young Children.* Englewood Cliffs: Prentice-Hall, 1976.

Chomsky, N. *Language and the Mind.* New York: Harcourt, Brace, Jovanovich, 1968.

Eimas, P. D., Siueland, E. R., Jusczk, P., and Vigouto, J. "Speech Perception in Infants," in L. J. Stone et al., eds., *The Competent Infant.* New York: Basic Books, 1973.

Erikson, E., *Childhood and Society.* New York: W. W. Norton, 1950.

Etzel, B. C., Gewirtz, J. L. "Modification of Caretaker-Maintained High Rate Operant Crying in 6- and 20-Week-Old Infant Extinction of Crying with Reinforcement of Eye Contact and Smiling." *Journal of Experimental Child Psychology,* 1976, **5**.

Fagan, J. F. "Infants' Recognition of Invariant Features of Faces." *Child Development,* 1976, **47**.

Friedlander, B. Z. "Receptive Language Development in Infancy: Issues and Problems," in L. J. Stone, et al., eds., *The Competent Infant*. New York: Basic Books, 1973.

Fitzgerald, H. E., Strommen, E. A., and McKinney, J. P. *Developmental Psychology*. Homewood, Ill.: Dorsey Press, 1977.

Gordon, I. *The Infant Experience*. Columbus, Ohio: Charles E. Merrill, 1975.

Hunt, J. McV. "Attentional Preference and Experience: I." *Journal of Genetic Psychology*, 1970, **27**.

Jersild, A. T., Telford, C. W., and Sawrey, J. M. *Child Psychology*, 7th ed. Englewood Cliffs: Prentice-Hall, 1975.

Kagan, J. "Attention and Psychological Change in the Young Child." *Science*, 1970, **14**.

Kagan, J. "The Baby's Elastic Mind." *Human Nature Magazine*, Jan. 1978.

Kagan, J. "Continuity in Cognitive Development During the First Year." *Merrill-Palmer Quarterly*, 1969, **22**.

Latif, I. "The Psychological Basis of Linguistic Development." *Psychological Review*, 1934, **41**.

Lenneberg, E. H. "Language Disorders in Childhood." *Harvard Review*, 1964, **34**.

Lewis, M. "The Busy, Purposeful World of a Baby." *Psychology Today*, Feb. 1977.

Maccoby, E., and Jacklin, C. N. *The Psychology of Sex Differences*. Stanford, Ca.: Stanford University Press, 1974.

MacFarlaine, A. "What a Baby Knows." *Human Nature Magazine*, Feb. 1978.

McNeill, D. "The Development of Language," in P. H. Mussen, ed., *Carmichael's Manual of Child Psychology*, Vol I. New York: John Wiley and Sons, 1970.

Moerk, E. "Principles of Interaction in Language." *Merrill-Palmer Quarterly*, 1972, **18**.

Moerk, E. "Processes of Language Teaching and Training in the Interactions of Mother-Child Dyads." *Child Development*, 1976, **47**.

Mundy-Castle, C. A., and Anglin, J. M. "Looking Strategies in Infants." in L. J. Stone, et al., eds., *The competent Infant*. New York: Basic Books, 1973.

Mussen, P. H., Congar, J. J., and Kagan, J. *Child Development and Personality*, 4th ed. New York: Harper & Row, 1974.

Nelson, K. "Structure and Strategy in Learning to Talk." *Monographs of the Society for Research in Child Development*, 1973, **37**.

Phillips, J. *The Origins of Intellect: Piaget's Theory*, 2d ed. San Francisco: W. H. Freeman, 1975.

Piaget, J. "Piaget's Theory," in P. H. Mussen, ed., *Carmichael's Manual of Child Psychology*, Vol 1, 3d ed. New York: John Wiley & Sons, 1970.

Piaget, J., and Inhelder, B. *The Psychology of the Child*. Translated by Helen Weaver. New York: Basic Books, 1969.

Samples, R. *The Metamorphic Mind*. Menlo Park, Ca.: Addison-Wesley, 1976.

Schultz, T. T., and Zigler, E. "Emotional Concomitants of Visual Mastery in Infants: The Effects of Stimulus Movement on Smiling and Vocalization." *Journal of Experimental Psychology*, 1970, **11**.

Schwartz, A., Rosenberg, D., and Brackbill, Y. "An Analysis of the Components of Social Reinforcement of Infant Vocalizations." *Psychonomic Science*, 1970, **20**.

Shachter, F. F., Marquis, R., Bundy, C., and McNair, J. "Everyday Speech Acts of Disadvantaged and Advantaged Mothers to Their Toddlers." Paper presented at the Biennial Meeting of the Society for Research in Child Development, New Orleans, March 1977.

Smith, M. E. "Measurement of Vocabulary of Young Bilingual Children in Both of the Languages Used." *Journal of Genetic Psychology*, 1949, **74**.

Snow, C. E. "Mothers' Speech to Children Learning Language." *Child Development*, 1972, **43**.

Wolff, P. H. "The Natural History of Crying and Other Vocalizations in Early Infancy," in L. J. Stone, et al., eds., *The Competent Infant*. New York: Basic Books, 1973.

White, B. *The First Three Years of Life*. Englewood Cliffs: Prentice-Hall, 1975.

Wolff, P. H. and Feinbloom, R. I. "Critical Periods and Cognitive Development in the First Two Years." *Pediatrics*, 1969, **44**, No. 6.

CHAPTER 9

Ainsworth, M. D., and Bell, S. M. "Attachment, Exploration and Separation, Illustrated by the Behavior of One-Year-Olds in a Strange Setting." *Child Development*, 1970, **41**, 49-67.

Ainsworth, M. D., and Wittig, B. A. "Attachment and Exploratory Behavior of One-Year-Olds," in B. M. Foss, ed., *Determinants of Infant Behavior*, Vol 4. New York: John Wiley & Sons, 1972.

Assagioli, R. *The Act of Will.* Baltimore: Penguin Books, 1973.

Assagioli, R. *Psychosynthesis: A Manual of Principles and Techniques.* New York: The Viking Press, 1965.

Bowlby, J. *Attachment.* New York: Basic Books, 1969.

Erikson, H. *Childhood and Society.* New York: W. W. Norton, 1950.

Goodenough, F. L. *Anger in Young Children.* Minneapolis: University of Minnesota Press, 1931.

Harlow, H. "The Nature of Love." *American Psychology*, 1958, **13**, 673-84.

Hendricks, G., and Wills, R. *The Centering Book.* Englewood Cliffs: Prentice-Hall, 1975.

Jersild, A., and Holmes, F. B. "Methods of Overcoming Children's Fears." *Journal of Psychology*, 1935, **1**, 75-104.

Leonard, G. B. *The Transformation.* New York: Dell, 1973.

Maslow, A. H. *Motivation and Personality.* New York: Harper & Row, 1970.

Maslow, A. H. *Toward a Psychology of Being.* New York: D. van Nostrand Company, 1968.

Robson, K. S. "The Role of Eye-to-Eye Contact in Maternal-Infant Attachment." *Journal of Child Psychology and Psychiatry*, 1967, **8**, 13-25.

Sears, R., Maccoby, E. E., and Levin, H. *Patterns of Child Rearing.* Evanston, Ill.: Row, Peterson and Co., 1957.

Smart, M. S., and Smart, R. C. *Infants.* New York: Macmillan, 1973.

Thomas, A., Chess, S., and Birch, H. G. "Origins of Personality," *Scientific American*, 1970, **223**, No. 2, 102-109.

von Franz, M. L. "The Process of Individuation," in C. G. Jung and others, *Man and His Symbols.* New York: Doubleday, 1964.

White, B. *The First Three Years of Life.* Englewood Cliffs: Prentice-Hall, 1975.

White, B., and Watts, J. C. *Experiences and Environment: Major Influences on the Development of the Young Child*, Vol I. Englewood Cliffs: Prentice-Hall, 1973.

Index

162

Perception: adaptive process of, 97; and caregiving, 36; and motor experience, 90, 92; and understanding, 112. *See also* Sensory abilities

Piaget, Jean: theory and intuitive experience, 115; object permanancy, 81; and sensory motor experience, 112. *See also* Mental development

Pikler, Emmi, M.D., mentioned, 11

Pincer grasp. *See* Motor development

Play: as curriculum, 70; adult role in, 48, 70; spontaneous, 17

Praise, using, 52, 53, 71

Problem solving: and education, 45; caregiver role in, 24, 71; facilitating, 24; mentioned, 10. *See also* Mental development

Pupillary reflex, early presence of, 95

Quality time: directed and undirected, 17; explained, 16; in feeding, 30-32; mentioned, 9

Readiness: in self help skills, 41; in learning social skills, 42

Record keeping: in infant centers, 66; to promote attachment, 68

Reflexes: development of, 98-101; and attachment, 79; thinking and understanding, 109; and sensory motor experience, 110

Relationship: development of, 10, 25; fostered through caregiving, 17, 26, 30-32, 42; and responsiveness, 12; mentioned, 26; described, 30; synchronous, 26. *See also* Attachment

Respect: as goal, 9, 12, 19; exercise, 19; illustrated, 17, 20-21, 42; and autonomy, 84; importance of, 131, 138, 140; shown in caregiving, 42; in diapering, 38; in dressing, 40; in feeding, 30-32; mentioned, 10, 26. *See also* Quality time; Relationship

Rewards: and undesirable behavior, 52; mentioned, 53

Security: at nap time, 41; mentioned, 10; source of, 25. *See also* Trust

Self: development of, 135; guides for fostering, 138; and infant needs, 136

Self-awareness, importance of, 6

Self-calming behaviors: examples of, 134; and development of self, 135

Self-help skills: readiness for, 41; bathing, 42

Sensory abilities: hearing, 92-94; taste and smell, 94; touch, 94-95; sight/vision, 95-97

Sensory motor experience: development of, 110-12; and language, 117

Sensory stimulation: mentioned, 92, 97; reactions at birth, 126

Separation: and trust, 25; and anxiety, 127

Sharing: taught by modeling, 54

Sleeping: determining need for, 42; and individual schedules, 41

Social skills, 42

Staff relations in infant center, 66

Stimulation, limits of, 44-45

"Stranger anxiety," 127

Stress: and infant education, 49-50; optimal level, 49; and development, 136-37; mentioned, 62

Sympathy: as reward, 24; disadvantage of, 21

Tactile perception. *See* Sensory abilities

Thumb sucking. *See* Self calming behaviors

Toys: at nap time, 41 mentioned, 10. *See also* Environment

Trust: and motor stability, 101; and attachment, 84; and self calming abilities, 135; mentioned, 10. *See also* Relationship

Values: exercise, 7-8; and quality time, 16; mentioned, 6; incorporating parents', 66; mentioned, 6

Vision. *See* Sensory abilities

Vocalization. *See* Communication